Contents

Foreword

A major part of my life has been devoted to raising standards of excellence in cooking, not just in my own kitchens but throughout Europe and world-wide, with the help of my competition the Bocuse d'Or. When I visited London to cook a special anniversary dinner for Michel Bourdin at the Connaught I was happy to see Charles Florman, whom I have known for many years. When he told me that he was planning to publish his personal guide to Europe's best restaurants I welcomed the project as it will draw attention to, and promote, the high standards of cooking that exist in so many restaurants today, and therefore I was happy to agree to write this foreword.

Until now there has been no pocket guide in English to restaurants in Europe. The purpose of this guide is to introduce the reader to the best food that Europe has to offer. It is important to highlight not only quality food but also outstanding service, ambience, table settings and wine lists. Business travellers and gourmets alike will find it extremely useful as it selects the most exceptional places to eat in each country. I am delighted to recommend this practical and informative guide to the reader.

Paul Bocuse
Lyon, August 2001

Bocuse d'Or (Golden Bocuse) is the world's leading cookery competition held every second year in Lyon. Chefs come from all over the world to compete, to show their skills, and to win the coveted medals. The next competition will be held in January 2003.

Introduction

The Florman Guide is a selection of the best restaurants in Europe. Having travelled extensively in Europe for many years I have developed a great passion for gastronomy. Through this I have come to know many of Europe's greatest chefs and have taken pleasure in following their progress to the top.

After so many years of enjoying haute cuisine at its best I decided to share my thoughts by writing the first pocket-size guide to Europe's top restaurants. I have created a star rating system over five levels with three stars being the highest quality. In determining the rating of a restaurant I take into account not only the quality of the cooking and presentation of dishes but of course the atmosphere, service and the wine list. Details of the five star rating system can be found at the beginning of this book. In addition, below the five levels of stars, I have listed good restaurants in many of Europe's most important cities even if they don't qualify for a star rating. These restaurants carry the 'o' symbol. This gives one indication as to the sort of guide this is: I am attempting to list good restaurants in all of Europe's most important cities, and so provide an essential aid to the traveller within Europe.

Within each town or city I have chosen restaurants that I consider to be the best and these I review in full. However there are also many establishments that I do not have space to review but deserve to be mentioned, and they are featured under the sub-heading 'Also recommended'. Perhaps in the next edition of the Florman Guide I will review them in full. I have also introduced the best restaurants known to me in the most important cities of Eastern Europe and the United States.

This book is not only a restaurant guide; I have also included several articles, written by friends of mine who are experts in their field, on such subjects as truffles, wine, champagne and cigars; which I hope will be of interest. Finally, I have prepared three gourmet car trips through Europe which I hope many of my readers will have time to enjoy.

I hope you will enjoy the first edition of the Florman Guide to Europe's Best Restaurants and will find it a useful aid on your travels through Europe. I would welcome your comments and suggestions for our next edition.

Charles Florman
London, August 2001

The Author

Charles Florman is well qualified to write a guide to Europe's top restaurants. As a senior executive of one of America's top publishers for over 30 years and, as European Publisher of Fortune Magazine, he travelled internationally on a weekly basis and took every opportunity to sample the finest cuisine that Europe has to offer. As a result he has now eaten in practically every restaurant that has, or has ever had, the coveted three Michelin stars. While living in Sweden he became an agent for French quality wines and champagne and therefore acquired a considerable knowledge of good wines. The author is also a 'Chevalier de l'Ordre des Coteaux de Champagne' and formerly a 'Chevalier de Tastevin' in Burgundy.

In 1982 Charles Florman was invited by Egon Ronay to become a restaurant reviewer for his new European guide 'A Taste of Europe' and during the next 15 years he regularly reviewed restaurants and hotels in seven European countries. He has also contributed to Plaza & Janes' European Traveller's Guide. In 1983 he was a founder member of the British Academy of Gastronomes and is currently the British Academy's International Delegate. In 1999 he was the initiator and one of the organisers of an international gastronomic conference in London attended by delegates from 17 countries. Charles Florman's research is facilitated by the fact that he speaks 6 languages fluently.

Charles Florman is the founder and chairman of an exclusive dining club called Les Amis de 'C' with some 40 members which, on a monthly basis, samples the best cooking in London and other cities in Europe. Recently the author was also a judge at the final of the Master of Culinary Arts Restaurant Management & Service examinations in London. Charles lives in London with his wife Lili who is, incidentally, a very fine cook.

Editorial Advisory Board

As it is quite impossible to be up to date on the very latest developments in each of our restaurants a gastronomic adviser in each country has been appointed to keep the Florman Guides fully informed of recent developments. We have been fortunate in appointing a very distinguished group of leading gastronomes to this board. They are:

AUSTRIA: Count Johannes Walderdorff
President, Austrian Academy of Gastronomy

BENELUX: Kerstin Norberg
Board member, Club Royale de Gastronomes de Belgique

DENMARK: Jørgen Fakstorp
Keeper of the Records, Danish Academy of Gastronomy

FRANCE: Michel Genin
President, International Academy of Gastronomy, Paris

GERMANY: Knut Guenther
President, German Academy of Gastronomy

GREAT BRITAIN & IRELAND: Andrew Eliel
Former Editorial Director of the Egon Ronay Guides

GREECE: Ari Sofianos
Founder, Greek Academy of Gastronomy

ITALY & SWITZERLAND: Giuseppe Tomé
Member of the Board, Accademia Italiana della Cucina and member Swiss Academy of Gourmets

SWEDEN, NORWAY & FINLAND:
Gunnar Forssell
Master Chef and member, Swedish Gastronomic Academy

SPAIN & PORTUGAL: Don Rafael Anson
President, Spanish Academy of Gastronomy

Austria (+43)

Vienna

Drei Husaren ★

Weihburggasse 4
Tel: 01 51 21 09 20 Fax: 01 51 21 09 218
The Three Hussars specialises in Viennese dishes. Founded by three cavalry officers in the 1930's this restaurant has had its ups and downs but is now under the competent management of Uwe Kohl. It is one of the most popular eating and meeting places, especially after an evening out at the opera or a concert and is well situated opposite St Stephen's cathedral. The restaurant is intimate and in the evening there is piano music. Reservations are essential as Drei Husaren is especially popular with tourists.

Korso in Hotel Bristol ★

Kärntner Ring 1
Tel: 01 51 51 65 46 Fax: 01 51 51 65 50
(Closed Saturday lunch)
Next to the opera you will find a luxury restaurant with good all round cooking thanks to chef Reinhard Gerer, one of Vienna's finest. He trained in Munich with famous chefs Eckart Witzigmann and Heinz Winkler. The menu offers many Austrian dishes but also some international haute cuisine. I can recommend calves' kidneys with mustard and chives, crispy roast duck, and roasted sole with a tomato and olive sauce.

Palais Schwarzenberg O

Schwarzenbergplatz 9
Tel: 01 798 4515 Fax: 01 798 4714
The setting is magnificent. Here is an 18th century Baroque palace in a vast private park with fountains and statues. This palace is now a luxurious hotel with an excellent terrace restaurant which overlooks the park. In winter the restaurant moves into the main sitting room and meals are served near the open fire. Chef Gerhard Klambauer likes to serve dishes that compliment the elegance of the surroundings, such as risotto with spinach and black truffles, grilled turbot with potato ravioli and quail in a mushroom sauce. This is one of my favourite places to have lunch when I am in Vienna.

Steirereck ★★

Rasumofskygasse 2
Tel: 01 713 3168 Fax: 01 713 5182
(Closed Saturday & Sunday)

Most journalists and observers, and indeed the customers, rate this gastronomic restaurant the finest in Vienna. The exterior is not impressive but once inside you will find an attractive flower-filled dining room. The service is impeccable and you will soon be offered bread from a special bread trolley filled with freshly baked loaves. Famous chef, Helmut Österreicher has now retired and is succeeded by Heinz Reitbauer Junior, son of the owners Heinz and Margarete. Heinz Jr has trained in some of the great restaurants in Europe which shows in the quality of the food. The cooking is also inspired by the southern Austrian province of Styria. The wine service is in the hands of sommelier Adolf Schmid, who has been responsible for the 30,000 bottle cellar for many years. Here are two dishes to try: turbot in an avocado crust and quail in red wine sauce. Reservations necessary.

Walter Bauer ★

Sonnenfelsgasse 17
Tel & Fax: 01 512 9871
(Closed mid-July - mid-August, Saturday & Monday lunch)

Vienna-born head chef Christian Domschitz cooks with creativity and originality in the attractive 17th century house with high vaulted ceilings and bay windows with rose-coloured walls. This restaurant is a good example of the high gastronomic standards now prevailing in Vienna. Some of the very fine dishes that I have noticed on the menu are gingerbread soufflé with Traminer sabayon, cream of chestnut soup with truffles, filet of sander in a sesame crust and venison and Tyrolean ham with pumpkin and celery mayonnaise.

Also recommended:

Café Demel FF

Kohlmarkt 14
Tel: 01 533 5516 Fax: 01 535 1717 26

The most famous patisserie of them all. Go morning or afternoon for coffee, tea and superb pastries.

Zimmerman O

Armbrustergasse 3-5
Tel: 01 370 2211 Fax: 01 370 6130

In the Heuriger wine district Zimmerman is special - a series of old vintners'cottages set in spacious gardens serving wine.

Salzburg

Goldener Hirsch ★

Getreidegasse 37

Tel: 06 6280 840 Fax: 06 6284 3349

Salzburg, a lovely town with churches and castles, surrounded by beautiful countryside, is an essential destination for all music lovers, especially fans of Mozart. My favourite place to stay is the historic Goldener Hirsch (golden stag) in possibly the oldest building in Salzburg, an 800 year-old patrician house with vaulted halls and enchanting rooms. The restaurant serves good Austrian food such as venison with red cabbage and their speciality Crepe Goldener Hirsch. There is an extensive wine list of both Austrian and French wines. The owner, Count Johannes Walderdorff, keeps standards high and will give you a friendly welcome.

Werfen

Obauer ★★

Markt 46

Tel: 06468 52 120 Fax: 06468 52 1212

(Closed Monday & Tuesday)

Not far from Salzburg (30 kms south) is one of the finest restaurants in Austria enjoying an international reputation for quality food. Karl and Rudolf Obauer offer their clients top class Austrian cuisine with French overtones in a restored 15th century historic house with two dining rooms and a terraced garden. The menu matches the elegant surroundings. Some examples include red-bellied lake trout and calves' head vinaigrette. For a dessert try plum soufflé with poppy seeds. There are eight bedrooms for those guests who want to stay overnight for another meal. Why not do so when the culinary standard is so high.

Belgium (+32)

Brussels

Bruneau ★★★

Avenue Broustin 75
Tel: 02 427 6978 Fax: 02 425 9726
(Closed Tuesday dinner, Wednesday & August)
One of only two three star restaurants in Brussels is located some distance from the centre, but don't miss it. Jean-Pierre Bruneau offers some interesting specialities such as carpaccio of scallops with goose liver, lobster with truffles and sea bass with caviar. The recently refurbished interior is attractive and modern with soft beige and yellow. There is a shaded terrace outside.

Claude Dupont ★★

Avenue Vital Riethuisen 46
Tel: 02 426 0000 Fax: 02 426 6540
(Closed Monday, Tuesday & July)
A warm and welcoming town house restaurant under the management of Claude Dupont and his son Eric. Chef/patron Claude is a very fine chef, definitely among the top in Brussels. His speciality is game and during the winter season the menu will feature saddle of venison and wild duck. Other dishes that I have enjoyed here are grilled perch-pike and succulent roast lamb with a mustard crust and herbs. There is a good wine list dominated by Bordeaux wines. Claude and Eric deserve their two stars.

Comme Chez Soi ★★★

Place Rouppe 23
Tel: 02 512 2921 Fax: 02 511 8052
(Closed Sunday, Monday & July)
Proprietor Pierre Wynants is easily the most famous Chef in Belgium and you have to book way ahead to be seated in the very attractive but small Art Nouveau interior by the renowned architect Horta. As the dining room is limited to some 40 seats M and Mme Wynants have opened up an extension to their kitchen where favoured guests can sit and watch the chefs at work. Recently 15 members of my dining club travelled from London to Brussels to enjoy a superb lunch in the kitchen. After a glass of Champagne in the vast wine cellar below the restaurant we sat down to oyster consommé, grilled turbot, duck in Chambertin and mango sorbet.

De Bijgaarden ★★1/2

Van Beverenstraat 20
Tel: 02 466 4485 Fax: 02 463 0811
(Closed Saturday lunch & Sunday & 3 weeks in August)
On the edge of Brussels and facing the castle of Groot Bijgaarden this restaurant is a delight. It takes some 20-25 minutes by car to reach this gastronomic haven from the centre of Brussels but on arrival you can relax on the terrace overlooking the countryside and then eat in an elegant and sumptuous dining room. Proprietor Willy Vermeulen and chef Olivier Schlissinger will look after your culinary needs with, for example, turbot château with Bearnaise sauce or oven-roasted poularde with morels. I can particularly recommend grilled Colchester oysters with a truffled vinaigrette. Surely Olivier must be on the way to his third star - we will see next year.

La Maison du Cygne FF

Grand Place 9
Tel: 02 511 8244 Fax: 02 514 3148
(Closed Saturday lunch & Sunday & 3 weeks in August)
A very fashionable 'in' place right on the famous Grand Place where everybody congregates. 'The House of the Swan' has a very elegant oak-panelled interior from where you can watch what is going on in the square below. As the cooking has recently improved I recommend it for an evening out in central Brussels. The wine cellar is remarkable, containing some 70,000 bottles.

L'Ecailler du Palais Royal ★★

Rue Bodenbroek 18
Tel: 02 512 8751 Fax: 02 511 9950
(Closed Sunday & August)
In a good location facing the church of Notre-Dame du Sablon L'Ecailler is without doubt one of the best seafood restaurants in Belgium. Be sure to try their oysters, either from Colchester or Zeland, followed by lobster or turbot or monkfish. Proprietor Rene Falke and his chef Atillio Basso offer the freshest shellfish and fish that can be found. The desserts are of a high standard.

Maison du Boeuf ★

Hilton Hotel, Boulevard de Waterloo 38
Tel: 02 504 1334 Fax: 02 504 2111
(Closed Saturday lunch, Sunday & mid-July - mid-August)
On the first floor of the first class Hilton hotel is an excellent restaurant, the Maison du Boeuf, and of course it specialises in the finest beef, such as roast beef in a crust of salt which I have tried - delicious. Chef Michel Theurel does of course present a varied cuisine and among other interesting dishes are rack of lamb and sea bass with thyme and during the season several good game dishes. The wine list has a good choice from the new world and is good value. If you sit by the window you can take in the panoramic view of the park below.

Sea Grill ★★

Fossé-aux-Loups 47
Tel: 02 227 3120 Fax: 02 219 6262
(Closed Saturday lunch, Sunday & 3 weeks in July/August)
One of Brussels' best restaurants is to be found in the Hotel Radisson SAS. The interior is dominated by vast etched-glass murals and as the name suggests specialities are products from the sea. Young chef Yves Mattagne has a high reputation and I can recommend steamed scallops, baked sea bass with truffles and line-caught sea bass in a salt crust.

Villa Lorraine ★

Avenue du Vivier d'Oie 75
Tel: 02 374 3163 Fax: 02 372 0195
(Closed Sunday & 3 weeks in July)
For many years Villa Lorraine was not only the most famous but also the best restaurant in Brussels. Luxurious and attractive it is situated away from the centre adjoining the Bois de le Cambre. Chef/proprietor Freddy Vandecasserie offers a most varied and extensive menu and a fine wine list. The best place to enjoy your meal is on the terrace. I have enjoyed many an excellent evening here.

Also recommended:

Aux Armes de Bruxelles O

Rue Bouchers 13
Tel: 02 511 5598 Fax: 02 514 3381
The narrow streets leading off the Grand Place are lined with restaurants. This is one of the best with many specialities and quite reasonably priced.

La Truffe Noire ★

Boulevard de la Cambre 12
Tel: 02 640 4422 Fax: 02 647 9704
An elegant restaurant with Italian and French cuisine specialising in truffles, both black and white.

Antwerp

't Fornuis ★1/2

Reyndersstraat 24
Tel: 03 233 6270 Fax: 03 233 9903
(Closed Saturday, Sunday & 3 weeks in August)
In a 17th century house with a rather rustic Flanders interior you will find possibly the best restaurant in Antwerp. Chef/patron Johan Segers is a dynamic character who will personally discuss the choice of dishes with his guests rather than present a menu. Among his many interesting dishes are oysters in a seawater jelly with caviar or fresh crab in a herb pancake with lobster sauce. A good main course is roast pigeon with peas and onions; and why not order Mirabelle plums flambéed in eau de vie for your dessert. The restaurant seats only 30 so do ring and reserve your table.

Also recommended

De Matelote ★

Haarstraat 9
Tel: 03 231 3207 Fax: 03 231 0813
Housed in an elegant 16th century building this restaurant has excellent seafood but only 25 seats so do book early.

Bruges

De Karmeliet ★★★

Langestraat 19

Tel: 050 33 82 59 Fax: 050 33 10 11

(Closed Sunday lunch & Monday)

In the Flemish region of Belgium, called Flanders, the leading chef is Geert van Hecke. His restaurant can be found in the charming town of Bruges, near the coast (sometimes called the 'Venice of the north' because of its many canals). Chef van Hecke was trained by the late, great Alain Chapel and this shows in his very sophisticated cuisine. To experience his cooking my wife and I took the train from Brussels which takes less than an hour and it was well worth the journey. Formerly an elegant private house with a garden next to a canal, van Hecke converted it into a restaurant in the 1980's. We enjoyed our dinner very much and sampled dishes such as large roasted langoustines with a pasta salad, gâteau of cèpe mushrooms with scallops in almond pastry or noisettes of venison.

Noirefontaine

Auberge du Moulin Hideux ★

Route de Dohan 1

Tel: 061 467 015 Fax: 061 467 281

(Closed Wednesday lunch)

In southern Belgium, in the valley of Semois, near Luxembourg, this old mill house is a charming inn perfect for a weekend visit. Amusingly the name 'hideux' means hideous but that is far from the truth as the name actually comes from an old expression meaning 'two mills'. The food is of good one star quality. Chef Philippe Duret likes to prepare good simple food from local recipes, but also more complicated dishes such as roast pigeon and fried sea bass. Service is very friendly.

Luxembourg (+352)

Luxembourg

Le Patin d'Or ★

40 route de Bettembourg 40
Tel: 22 64 99 Fax: 40 40 11
(Closed Saturday & Sunday)

The setting of this restaurant is rather remote, deep inside the forest. Many tables are outside on the terrace, while others look out through vast windows. Chef/patron Michel Berring spent many years working with the famous Roger Vergé in France, and this shows in the quality of the food. On his repertoire are some good fish courses such as pan fried filet of red mullet and roasted sea bream on a bed of home made pasta with lobster flavoured olive oil.

Echternach

La Bergerie ★★

Geyershaff
Tel: 79 04 64 Fax: 79 07 71
(Closed Sunday dinner, Monday, January & February)

La Bergerie is to be found in the forest in an ancient farm-house. In the summer you can dine on the flower-filled terrace. In winter dinner will be served near the great fire-place. Thierry Phal and his wife have now taken over this first class restaurant with some very interesting dishes on the menu. Let me suggest coquilles St Jacques with truff-les or foie gras d'oie au naturel followed by agneau en croute aux almandes et pistaches. There is also a 'discove-ry' menu of five courses in smaller portions. This is without doubt one of the very best restaurants in Luxembourg, possibly the best. There is a hotel annexe with 15 rooms a short distance away - transfer by bus.

Denmark (+45)

Copenhagen

Kommandanten ★★

Ny Adelgade 7
Tel: 33 12 09 90 Fax: 33 93 12 23
(Closed Saturday lunch & Sunday)

Modern French cooking in an attractive 17th century town house sums up this excellent restaurant. Old wooden beams go well with the grey and cobalt interior. There is also Royal Copenhagen china and candles on the tables and, with creative lighting, a warm atmosphere exists. Young chef Mikkel Maarbjerg took over two years ago and offers many interesting classic French dishes. I can recommend quails crepinette with asparagus, carpaccio of scallops and other seafood dishes. Desserts include strawberry tart with white wine jelly and vanilla ice cream.

Kong Hans Kaelder ★★

Vingårdsstraede 6
Tel: 33 11 68 68 Fax: 33 32 67 68
(Closed Sunday & July)

The old gothic wine cellar which is the King Hans restaurant is one of the most famous and one of the best restaurants in Copenhagen. I often go there on my visits to this charming city and although the acoustics can be difficult it is nice to sit under the vaults and enjoy a very good meal. For over twenty years the chef was French but now Thomas Rode Anderson has taken over and keeps up the standard. The highest cookery award in Denmark is the Champagne prize, created and funded by five famous Champagne houses. In 2001 the award has been given to the Kong Hans Kaelder for its high standard and superlative cuisine. Chef Thomas Rode can be proud of his achievement.

Krogs Fiskerestaurant FF

Gammel Strand 38
Tel: 33 15 89 15 Fax: 33 15 83 19
(Closed Sunday)

Krogs is the place for the lover of fish and shellfish. Facing the harbour it is an elegant and classic restaurant offering a great variety of seafood, mostly from Danish waters. The interior has been recently restored to its original style from the beginning of the last century. One dish that I have enjoyed here was braised turbot with lobster mousse and

glazed mushrooms. Naturally herrings, Danish shrimps and langoustines will always be on the menu and their lobster dishes are excellent. An amusing dessert is a marzipan soufflé with candied cherries and sorbet. The wine list is extensive and very good.

Le Sommelier

O

Bredgade 63-65
Tel: 33 11 45 15 Fax: 33 11 59 79
(Closed Saturday lunch, Sunday & July)

As the name indicates Le Sommelier has until recently been predominately a wine bar with brasserie type food. However the arrival last year of well-known chef Francis Cardenau has resulted in much higher gastronomic standards. Wines are still the heart and soul of the Sommelier with over 900 different wines listed, of which 30 are served by the glass. The location on Bredgade is very central.

Lumskebugten

FF

Esplanaden 21
Tel: 33 15 60 29 Fax: 33 32 87 18
(Closed Saturday lunch & Sunday)

There is a certain relaxed atmosphere here that draws me to this brasserie in a nineteenth century pavilion, only a stone's throw from the harbour. It has long been a favourite of mine especially in clement weather when lunch is served out of doors, while in the evening tables are candlelit. The cooking is Danish with French overtones concentrating on fish and shellfish. Good value.

Nouvelle

★

Gammel Strand 34
Tel: 33 13 50 18 Fax: 33 32 07 97
(Closed Saturday lunch & Sunday)

Beside the canal on the first floor of a building from the 19th century, Nouvelle has an elegant interior and a welcoming atmosphere. In the summer there is dining outdoors. The cooking is Scandinavian with many excellent fish dishes. Some of these are mussels gratinée, North Sea turbot, either grilled or poached, and lobster fricasée with green apples and curry hollandaise. For those in a spending mood Nouvelle offers a special caviar menu which I intend to try on my next visit.

Pierre André ★

Ny Østergade 21

Tel: 33 16 17 19 Fax: 33 16 17 72

(Closed Saturday lunch, Sunday & 3 weeks in July/August)

As the name indicates this a French restaurant in the very centre of Copenhagen, next to the popular shopping street Strøget. Chef/proprietor Philippe Houdet and his wife, Sussie, assisted by French staff, opened for business only 5 years ago but have gained a good reputation for their quality food. The restaurant is named after their two small sons. Phillipe and Sussie regularly travel to southern Europe to bring back new ideas and new products. Among items on the menu are dill-marinated wild Irish salmon and lobster with apple-horseradish coulis, and roe deer with fruit and fall vegetables and sauce poivrade.

Also Recommended:

Era Ora ★

Overgaden neden Vandet 33b

Tel: 32 54 06 93 Fax: 32 96 02 09

Probably the best Italian restaurant in Copenhagen - good anti-pasti platter.

Ida Davidsen O

St. Kongensgade 70

Tel: 33 91 36 55 Fax: 33 11 36 55

The most famous - and the best - Danish sandwich restaurant (in Danish 'Smorrebrod') open from10am to 4pm only.

Leonore Christine FF

Nyhavn 9

Tel & Fax: 33 13 50 40

Small and charming restaurant in a listed building, overlooking the Nyhavn (new harbour) canal.

Near Copenhagen

Den Gule (Yellow) Cottage O

Strandvejen 506

Tel: 39 64 06 91 Fax: 39 64 27 77

A small attractive seaside restaurant, a few kilometres north of Copenhagen. Good French-inspired cooking.

Ålsgårde

Jan Hurtigkarl ★

Nordro Strandvej 154
Tel: 49 70 90 03 Fax: 49 70 97 93
(Only open April - September, closed Monday)
Jan Hurtigkarl is one of the best restaurants along the coast north of Copenhagen. The Hurtigkarl family, father and son, have been leading chefs and restaurateurs in Copenhagen for many years but some time ago Jan, the son, opened his own place. On my last visit I sat on the covered terrace while enjoying my meal and enjoyed the calming view over the sea towards the coast of Sweden. Jan's cooking is international but, as is quite usual in Scandinavia, fish courses dominate. I had lobster and artichoke hearts followed by braised lamb with a spicy sauce, ending with almond cream in meringue with marinated berries. After the meal you might enjoy Jan's private bowling alley, open to the guests!

Hellerup

Saison ★1/2

Hellerup Park Hotel, Strandvejen 203
Tel: 39 62 48 42 Fax: 39 62 20 30
(Closed Sunday & 3 weeks in July)
Erwin Lauterbach is one of the finest chefs in Denmark. I have followed his career for many years and have had the pleasure of noting his success and enjoying his cooking. Erwin runs this French/Danish gourmet restaurant, located in the Hellerup Park Hotel, only 5 kms north of Copenhagen, along the coast road. The menu is changed daily, depending on the produce at the daily market. Erwin and his chef de cuisine Michael Kock use a lot of vegetables and cook with virgin oil, thereby reducing the use of butter in their dishes. There is a vegetarian menu available. Saison also has special gourmet menus. The hotel has 71 bedrooms and also a simpler Italian restaurant, Via Appia.

Millinge

Falsled Kro ★★

Assenvej 513
Tel: 62 68 11 11 Fax: 62 68 11 62
(only open May - September)
In the whole of Denmark there is no finer inn to visit than Falsled Kro on the island of Fyn halfway between Copenhagen and Jutland. There are only 11 rooms and

8 suites in this idyllic 15th century hotel facing the sea. In the lobby there is a huge white fireplace open on four sides surrounded by low slung chairs The restaurant is one of the very best in the whole country. French-born chef and co-owner Jean Louis Lieffroy cooks to a two star standard and I have enjoyed many of his creations such as home smoked salmon and haddock with aubergine and caviar.

Odense

Marie Louise ★★

Vestergade 70-72
Tel: 66 17 92 95 Fax: 66 19 19 95
(Closed Sunday, Monday lunch)
There are a couple of outstanding French chefs who have established themselves in Denmark. One of them is Michel Michaud whom I have had the pleasure of meeting several times when he was Chef de Cuisine in leading restaurants in Copenhagen and Millinge. A few years ago he and his wife, Annick, moved to Odense and opened Marie Louise, a restaurant with a high gastronomic standard. It was elected best restaurant in Denmark in 1999. The food is modern French and dishes worth mentioning are pot au feu of quail and langoustine ravioli in a bouillon with coriander as starters. For a main course try saddle of lamb with apple chutney and a good dessert is caramelised pancakes with Suzette sauce.

Søllerød

Søllerød Kro FF

Søllerødvej 35
Tel: 45 80 25 05 Fax: 45 80 22 70
An old favourite of mine in a pretty village 15 kilometers (9 miles) north of Copenhagen. The restaurant is in a 17th century thatched inn opposite the church. There are several attractive dining rooms filled with antiques and good paintings. The cuisine is French inspired and excellent. The desserts are particularly good and the wine list is quite extensive. Chef Casper Vedel's dishes include creamy apple herrings with horseradish and roasted rye bread and whole sole roasted in butter served with lemon and parsley cream. For dessert you could try pineapple marinated in basil served with honey and pine-nut ice cream. This is a perfect place for an excursion from Copenhagen.

Finland (+358)

Helsinki

Alexander Nevski FF

Pohjoisesplanadi 17
Tel: 09 639 610 Fax: 09 631 435
(Closed Sunday lunch)

Finland's long association with its giant neighbour Russia is reflected in many Russian dishes being available in Finnish restaurants. Overlooking the harbour, Alexander Nevski is located in a 19th century former Tsarist nobleman's house - a good setting for an enjoyable meal in Russian style. A dish I have enjoyed there is Beef Stroganoff and also the more Finnish version, Reindeer Stroganoff.

Chez Dominique ★

Ludvikinkatu 3
Tel: 09 612 7393 Fax: 09 612 44220
(Closed Sunday, Monday & July)

It is only three years ago that Chez Dominique opened its doors. There is only room for 36 guests in this intimate restaurant so do make a reservation. It is in the centre of Helsinki near the Esplanadi Park. Chef Hans Välimäki has quickly established a fine reputation and this was recognised when Chez Dominique was chosen as Restaurant of the Year in 2000 by the Gastronomic Society of Finland. On the current menu are some tempting dishes. Here are a few to consider: grilled scallops with olive powder or braised lobster with fried duck foie gras and as a main course halibut braised in anchovy butter. There are many good sweet wines to go with your dessert.

Havis Amanda ★

Unioninkatu 23
Tel: 09 666 882 Fax: 09 631 435
(Closed Sunday September - May)

Famous, traditional. and very good - that's Havis Amanda, the seafood specialist in Helsinki. It is of course appropriately situated by the harbour. The name relates to a statue of a young girl in a nearby boulevard, but the restaurant was originally started some 26 years ago by Finnish industry to support the country's fishermen and products of the sea are therefore what you will find here, presented by new chef Jurki Linna Huunnila. One dish I particularly want to mention, which happens to be a personal favourite, is bleak roe, the famous Nordic pink caviar, available only in Finland and Sweden. The eggs are very small because the

fish is small, but in this part of the world it is considered second only to Russian caviar. It is usually served on fried bread or toast with sour cream. A glass of aquavit is a good accompaniment. Skål!

G. W. Sundmans ★

Eteläranta 16

Tel: 09 622 6410 Fax: 09 661 331

Slightly salted arctic char with crayfish salad, breast of pheasant flavoured with green pepper, roasted noisette and chop of reindeer with morels in cream with port followed by soufflé of mangoes with raspberry sorbet. Does that not sound tempting? The chef who is responsible for these delicacies is one of the few women chefs cooking to star quality, Jarmo Vähä-Savo. She and her staff deliver these dishes on the first floor of a 19th century empire house with a view over the market square and with tiled stoves and paintings on the ceiling.

Also recommended:

George ★

Kalevankatu 17

Tel: 09 647 662 Fax: 09 647 110

Aubergine soup with morels, whitefish with spinach and sauce beurre-blanc are just two of the specialities of this small first class restaurant in the heart of Helsinki.

Kämp O

Kämp Hotel, Pohjoisesplanadi 29

Tel: 09 57 61 19 10 Fax: 09 57 61 22

An elegant restaurant in the newly refurbished Kämp hotel; excellent all round cooking.

Restaurant Lyon FF

Mannerheimintie 56

Tel: 09 408 131 Fax: 09 442 074

A friendly, French inspired neighbourhood restaurant facing the Opera House. Good French-style food, reasonably priced.

Restaurant Palace O

Eteläranta 10

Tel: 09 134 561 Fax: 09 654 786

The Palace complex consists of a hotel on the 9th floor, a first class restaurant on the 10th with a roof terrace on the 11th floor (with service) and a simpler restaurant, Palacenranda on the 2nd floor.

France (+33)

Paris

Alain Ducasse ★★★

Hôtel Plaza Athénée, 25 avenue Montaigne, 75008
Tel: 01 53 67 66 65 Fax: 01 53 67 66 66
(Closed for lunch except Thursday & Friday and closed Sunday)

Alain Ducasse, one of the most talked about chefs in France, is in the news again. Last year he was the only chef with two three star restaurants in the Michelin Guide but suddenly a star has gone in Monte Carlo. He may be spreading his talents too thin with more than half a dozen restaurants around the world. In Paris, however, he has successfully moved his establishment to the Hotel Plaza Athenée. The transfer has gone well partly thanks to the many staff members who have come along, such as chef du cuisine Jean François Piège and sommelier Gérard Margeon. Plaza Athenée has recently been restored at vast expense and the elegance of this magnificent hotel is well matched by Ducasse's luxury restaurant. Everything on the menu is interesting but let me mention crayfish en gratin, soup of morel mushrooms, asparagus and chicken breast with Albufera sauce. The wine list is of course magnificent.

Les Ambassadeurs ★★

Hôtel Crillon, 10 place Concorde, 75008
Tel: 01 44 71 15 00 Fax: 01 44 71 15 02

History and style combine in the perfect location! Les Ambassadeurs, a former ballroom, is a very beautiful restaurant in the historic 18th century Hotel Crillon. The Taittinger Champagne family are the owners and maintain impeccable standards. The restaurant's interior, in marble, with many chandeliers and mirrors makes every meal dramatic. Chef Dominic Bouchet offers a menu to match the surroundings. We could for example start with scallops carpaccio with a medley of fruits and black truffles and then move on to sea bass with aromatic herbs and shellfish in a wine broth. An unusual meat course would be saddle of rabbit with rosemary jus and fricassee of wild mushrooms. Of the many desserts I will mention just chocolate millefeuille with caramelised apples. The service is of

course impeccable. There is a reasonably priced lunch menu to offset the inevitably high à la carte prices.

L'Ambroisie ★★★

9 place des Vosges, 75004
Tel: 01 42 78 51 45
(Closed Sunday, Monday & August)

Chef/proprietor Bernard Pacaud is the classic 3 star chef, considered to be at the very top of his profession. Madame Danielle Pacaud is a charming hostess. With its location in eastern Paris on the beautiful Place des Vosges it is worth the trip. Not that long ago President and Mme Chirac chose L'Ambroisie to entertain Bill & Hilary Clinton there. Incidentally close to one thousand press, security and onlookers filled the Place outside! When you visit try foie gras with morels or coddled eggs with asparagus in sabayon sauce.

Amphyclès ★★

78 avenue des Ternes 75017
Tel: 01 40 68 01 01 Fax: 01 40 68 91 88
(Closed Saturday lunch and Sunday)

This restaurant deserves to be better known. It is a calm, relaxed place where chef Philippe Groult, who worked for ten years side-by-side with the famous Joël Robuchon, creates many attractive dishes such as omble chevalier du lac and duckling a la broche and coriandre. For dessert try caramelised pineapple or a pyramid of bitter chocolate with bananas flambée and cherries. I have decided to award Philippe Groult two stars and will follow him closely over the next year.

Apicius ★★

122 avenue Villiers 75017
Tel: 01 43 80 19 66 Fax: 01 44 40 09 57
(Closed Saturday, Sunday & August)

It is well worth going slightly out of the centre of Paris to experience the fine cooking of Jean Pierre Vigato, a self-taught chef. In a contemporary / modern interior with abstract art on the walls he serves both classic and inventive dishes. I have enjoyed many a good meal here and recommend you try the langoustines tempura and escalopes of duck foie gras with a sweet sour sauce. A good fish dish is roasted turbot. Desserts, many with chocolate, are a speciality, among them a superb chocolate soufflé.

Arpège ★★★

84 rue Varenne, 75007
Tel: 01 45 51 47 33 Fax: 01 44 18 98 39
(Closed Saturday and Sunday)

This is the smallest of the eight three star restaurants in Paris and until now has always been booked far ahead. It will be interesting to see if this will continue as chef/patron Alain Passard has recently announced to the world that he and his team are going vegetarian. This is a brave and most unusual move that has never been done before by a top establishment. Passard has quite simply decided that he prefers to cook vegetables and fish and that he will give up meat except for chicken. Why not find out for yourself what a top chef can achieve giving himself such limitations. Centrally placed almost opposite the Rodin museum, you descend narrow stairs to choose your menu, which might include medallions of homard and navets with honey and sherry vinegar.

Le Bristol ★★★

112 rue du Fbg Saint-Honoré, 75008
Tel: 01 53 43 43 40 Fax: 01 53 43 43 01

Although many Paris hotels have very good dining rooms I am limiting my choice to just a couple. With an excellent location on the shopping street of Faubourg de St Honoré and only a stone's throw from the Presidential palace the Bristol has top class accommodation. General manager Jean-Louis Souman is a good host and runs a very efficient hotel. The summer restaurant overlooks the garden so that you can enjoy chef Eric Frechon's cooking in a relaxed atmosphere. On a recent visit with friends Eric gave us croustillons de langoustine, sea bass with shellfish and an excellent riz de veau (sweetbread). An excellent dessert to try is soufflé a la noisette. Another time I had homard rafraîchi d'un gaspacho a l'huile d'olive , followed by pigeon vendéen, and ended with biscuit mi-cuit au chocolat grand cru with crème glacée. Frechon is a brilliant chef and I have decided to award him 3 stars.

Carré des Feuillants ★★

14 rue Castiglione 75001
Tel: 01 42 86 82 82 Fax: 01 42 86 07 71
(Closed Saturday lunch, Sunday & August)

Alain Dutournier is a leading representative of cooking from Gascony (South-West France) in Paris. He gets a strong two star rating for his fine dishes from his home

province, including of course foie gras. The restaurant is as much in the centre of Paris as it is possible to be, set in an arcade off the Rue de Rivoli. It is spacious and attractive with three dining rooms and a glass covered courtyard. On my last visit I enjoyed foie gras with truffles followed by roasted langoustines and then grilled duck. My friends ordered oysters followed by scallops. A dessert not to be missed is millefeuille with raspberries or other berries in season.

Copenhague ★

142 avenue Champs-Elysées, 75008
Tel: 01 44 13 86 26 Fax: 01 42 25 83 10
(Closed Saturday lunch & Sunday)

Would you like a Danish meal in the centre of Paris? Here it is waiting for you right on the Champs-Elysées in a complex of three restaurants from inexpensive to deluxe. It is owned by a Swedish friend of mine, Lennart Engstrom who carefully preserves Danish culinary traditions. The Copenhague on the first floor provides the finest Danish food outside Denmark. The Flora Danica on the ground floor offers terrace dining in the summer and there is also a simpler restaurant and a take-away. In Copenhague the finest Scandinavian produce is served, especially from the sea, such as salmon in many variations as well as herring. Prawns and crayfish are specialities. To accompany these dishes try a glass of Danish aquavit and of course Danish beer.

Faugeron ★★1/2

52 rue Longchamp, 75116
Tel: 01 47 04 24 53 Fax: 01 47 55 62 90
(Closed Saturday lunch, Sunday & August)

For many years Faugeron has been one of the finest two star restaurants in Paris and I have no hesitation in awarding Henri Faugeron an extra half-star. Just wait until you've tried his starter speciality - a soft-boiled egg with pureed truffles and brioche 'soldiers' and you may well think he is ready for his third star. Madame Gerlinde Faugeron is one of the finest hostesses in Paris and always welcomes you with a smile. Other dishes to try are a straightforward terrine of foie gras de canard and a tartare of coquille St Jacques also with truffles. Why not round off this meal with a mouth watering millefeuille au fraise. The sommelier, Mr Jambon, will help you select the right wine.

Grand Vefour

★★★

17 rue Beaujolais, 75001
Tel: 01 42 96 56 27 Fax: 01 42 86 80 71
(Closed Friday dinner, Saturday, Sunday & August)

The opulence of the lavish 18th century interior of Grand Vefour is hard to beat and many a famous name has admired its glorious décor : Napoleon Bonaparte, Jean Cocteau and Victor Hugo among others. Each table bears the name of a famous personality who has eaten there. It is dining at its most luxurious and the elegant setting with the chandeliers and mirrors has not changed much in the last two centuries since its opening in 1784. It has always been one of my favourite eating places in Paris since my first visit some 40 years ago. Chef Guy Martin, who comes from the Savoy region, has gone from strength to strength and last year joined a small group of three star holders in Paris. What is on his current menu? You could start with homard de Bretagne á oseille avec son jus followed by filet de Saint-Pierre meuniere with jus de coquillages; or try the tranche d'agneau with a café-chocolat jus. The Taittinger Champagne family are the owners and are also regular clients and therefore ensure a superb wine list.

Guy Savoy

★★

18 rue Troyon, 75017
Tel: 01 43 80 40 61 Fax:01 46 22 43 09
(Closed Saturday lunch, Sunday & 3 weeks in July/August)

The contemporary paintings are still there but last year the restaurant was completely redecorated transforming it into several smaller rooms with high quality leather and woodwork. Ever since he opened in the 1980's bearded Guy Savoy has been among the best known and most respected Paris chefs. As always in Paris you have to book well ahead for dinner in order to sample Savoy's many inventive dishes. Here are some examples I urge you to try, all of which I have enjoyed: duck foie gras with rock salt and duck jelly followed by saddle of veal lightly roasted with potato purée and truffles and for dessert vanilla millefeuille with fruit coulis.

Jamin

★★

32 rue Longchamps, 75116
Tel: 01 45 53 00 07 Fax: 01 45 53 00 15
(Closed Saturday, Sunday & 3 weeks in July/August))

This is the place where the great Joel Robuchon established his world reputation. Now that the master has gone his disciple Benoit Guichaud offers a modern classic cui-

sine of high quality. This is a calm restaurant for serious food lovers. Among dishes that we have eaten here are crème de laitue a la muscat, fricassee of langoustine in ravioli and grilled seabass with lobster butter. A dessert worth trying is poelée fraises a la fleur d'oranges and crème glacée. At lunch time there is a reasonably priced menu at around FF300 that I recommend.

Lucas Carton ★★★

9 place Madeleine, 75008
Tel: 01 42 65 22 90 Fax: 01 42 65 06 23
(Closed Saturday lunch, Sunday, Monday & 4 weeks in July/August)

This is one of the most historic restaurants in Paris. In the nineteenth century it was known as Lucas but in 1924 Frances Carton became the owner and thus was born Lucas Carton. In 1985 the famous chef Alain Senderens took over the stoves and from then on it was and still has three star cooking. The interior, very attractive, is both belle époque and art nouveau, with blond wood panelling and many mirrors. There are superb dishes such as Homard de Bretagne a la vanille, canard apicius rôti au miel, or perhaps steamed foie gras with cabbage; for dessert there is a really good millefeuille. Another way to dine here is to take the five-course menu accompanied by a glass of wine for each course, especially selected by the sommelier.

La Luna ★1/2

69 rue Rocher, 75008
Tel: 01 42 93 77 61 Fax: 01 40 08 0244
(Closed Sunday & August)

There are more good restaurants in Paris than anywhere else in the world, so how do you choose among the less well known? This is where the Florman guide comes to your assistance, with, for example, La Luna, a small hidden gem, only a short distance north of the centre. Owner Mme Katherine Delaunay offers a friendly reception. Chef Christian Rocher specialises in products from the sea; such as cold anchovy from Colliourle, fresh gambas in olive oil, dorade royal with ginger. La Luna is quite small so do phone ahead. It is open on Saturday for lunch, which is not so common in Paris.

Michel Rostang

★★1/2

20 rue Rennequin, 75017
Tel: 01 47 63 40 77 Fax: 01 47 63 82 75
(Closed Saturday lunch, Sunday and Monday)

Michel Rostang comes from a family of talented chefs. I used to know his father Jo (that's age for you!) who at one time had three Michelin stars in his restaurant on the Côte d'Azur. Michel's younger brother Philippe is still in charge in Antibes. Here in Paris Michel and his wife Marie-Claire are well- established in quietly elegant wood-panelled dining rooms with Lalique glass. Rostang is in the top group of Paris chefs as you will appreciate when experiencing dishes such as les rougets barbets pochés-rôtis or côte de veau de lait en casserole.

Paul Minchelli

★1/2

54 boulevard La Tour Maubourg, 75007
Tel: 01 47 05 89 86 Fax: 01 45 56 03 84
(Closed Sunday, Monday & August)

One of the great treats for a gourmet in France is to find a restaurant that serves sea urchins (oursin). Paul Minchelli, a great seafood specialist, serves these delicacies. The amber or coral roe of the female is very delicate with a drop of fresh lemon. Oysters, langoustines and grilled lobster are well presented here. One fish dish I recommend is Bar a la vapeur (steamed sea bass). These dishes do not come cheaply but it is also possible to eat in the bar where you can have one fish course and a glass of white wine, at a reasonable price. I did this on my last visit.

Pierre Gagnaire

★★★

Hôtel Balzac, 6 rue Balzac, 75008
Tel: 01 44 35 18 25 Fax: 01 44 35 18 37
(Closed Saturday & Sunday lunch)

Do you want to meet one of the greatest young chefs in France? Then make your way to the Hotel Balzac, a few steps off the Champs Elysees, where Pierre established himself after leaving his previous location in St Etienne near Lyon where there were simply not enough customers. I have followed Gagnaire's career for some time and eaten with him in both St Etienne and Paris. Not long ago I even took twenty friends from London with me to show them Pierre's talents. Many critics in France think he is at the very top of the gastronomic pyramid and I tend to agree. He specialises in offering many small dishes as a tasting menu. Here are two examples: langoustine, first grilled then minced into a mint cream bisque, and aiguillette (thin slices) of saddle of hare.

Port Alma ★1/2

10 avenue New-York, 75116
Tel: 01 47 23 75 11 Fax: 01 47 20 42 92
(Closed Sunday & Monday)
When I want to eat high quality seafood in a relaxed atmosphere I go to Port Alma, located appropriately next to the river Seine. Less known than more famous places I want to bring it to my readers' attention for its excellent produce. The oysters and lobsters are of course the best and freshest there are. Paul Caval also serves well prepared turbot and other white fish. On my last visit I finished with a chocolate soufflé and balanced the sweetness with a double espresso. During the week there is a lunch menu which was, until recently, only FF200.

Sormani ★

4 rue Géneral Lanrezac, 75017
Tel: 01 43 80 13 91 Fax: 01 40 55 07 37
(Closed Saturday, Sunday & 3 weeks in August)
If your thoughts are on Italian food while in Paris consider Sormani. It is quite possibly the best Italian restaurant in the capital. It is on a small side street near the Etoile. It is small but has recently been attractively redecorated. When I go there I like to start with either a carpaccio or a risotto or why not ravioli with black truffles if it's winter. Jean-Pascale Fayet keeps a high standard. It is fairly expensive for an Italian restaurant but there is a lunch menu which at least a couple of months ago was still FF250. Excellent wine list.

Taillevent ★★★

15 rue Lamennais, 75008
Tel: 01 44 95 15 01 Fax: 01 42 25 95 18
(Closed Saturday, Sunday & August)
Proprietor Jean-Claude Vrinat, whom I have known for many years, and young chef Michel Del Burgo form a great team in the attractive mansion that was once the home of Emperor Napoleon III. It is a perfect location for an important business lunch with both classic and modern cuisine and one of the finest and largest wine cellars with 350,000 bottles of quality wine. The service on my last visit was excellent. Del Burgo has modernised the menu and added some attractive new dishes such as cassolette de langoustine Bretonnes and agneau de lait rôti au thyme and afterwards a soufflé chaud au café.

La Tour d'Argent ★★★

15 quai Tournelle, 75005
Tel: 01 43 54 23 31 Fax: 01 44 07 12 04
(Closed Monday)

As you step out of the lift on the 6th floor to be greeted by your host Claude Terrail, owner and patron, as always with a blue carnation in his buttonhole, you are entering one of the most attractive dining rooms in Paris with a breathtaking view of the Seine and of Notre Dame. You will probably already have visited the wine museum and historic table settings on the ground floor. Since its opening in 1582 (!) this has been a favourite eating place for Parisians - and with good justification. And what about the food and wine? Relax. Chef Bernard Guilhaudin prepares with great skill the famous numbered duck à l'orange and many other specialities such as quenelles de brochet André Terrail and flambé de pêches à l'esprit de framboise with vanilla ice cream. On a recent visit I enjoyed duck aux cerise. The wine cellar of the Tour d'Argent has - wait for it - 500,000 bottles, the largest of any restaurant in the world. Sommelier Andrew Ridgeway will help you with your selection.

Also recommended:

Cantine des Gourmets ★

113 avenue La Bourdonnais, 75007
Tel: 01 47 05 47 96 Fax: 01 45 51 09 29

Popular and friendly with Provençale cooking. Conveniently open on Sundays

Le Divellec ★★

107 rue Université, 75007
Tel: 01 45 51 91 96 Fax: 01 45 51 31 75

This is the most famous and arguably the best fish restaurant in Paris but here the fish does not come cheap.

Lasserre ★★1/2

17 avenue F.D. Roosevelt, 75008
Tel: 01 4359 5343 Fax: 01 45 63 72 23

New chef Michel Roth is restoring this gastronomic temple to its former glory - and they still have the amazing roof that opens to clear the air and so allow the diners to watch the sky. Top class food in a luxury setting.

Jules Verne ★

2nd étage Tour Eiffel, 75007

Tel: 01 45 55 61 44 Fax: 01 47 05 29 41

Must be the best view in Paris - take the private lift to the second floor of the Eiffel Tower. Gourmet food in the sky. Essential to book well in advance.

Marius et Janette ★

4 avenue George V, 75008

Tel: 01 47 23 41 88 Fax: 01 47 23 07 19

A large and lively seafood restaurant well located on attractive Avenue Georges V. Very good choice of oysters.

Maxim's ★

3 rue Royale, 75008

Tel: 0142 65 27 94 Fax: 01 40 17 02 91

Famous for over a hundred years this luxurious establishment is now owned by Pierre Cardin. A very beautiful art nouveau dining room.

Pre Catelan ★★1/2

Route Suresnes, 75016

Tel: 01 44 14 4114 Fax: 01 45 24 43 25

Without doubt the best restaurant in the Bois de Boulogne. An attractive terrace for summer dining.

Les Trois Marches ★★

1 boulevard de la Reine, 78000

Tel: 01 39 50 13 21 Fax: 01 30 21 01 25

Excellent, luxurious. Definitely no.1 in Versailles.

Annecy

Auberge de l'Eridan (Marc Veyrat) ★★★

13 Vieille route des Pensières

Tel: 04 50 60 24 00 Fax: 04 50 60 23 63

(Only open May to November, closed Monday, Tuesday; Wednesday & Thursday lunch)

One of the very finest restaurants in France is to be found in an attractive small hotel on the eastern shores of Lake Annecy. To eat and stay there is something I recommend very highly. As you enter the large terrace restaurant you can see the water lapping the shore just below. When my wife and I stayed there we were able to swim in the lake before dinner. Above the restaurant are 11 comfortable bedrooms overlooking the water. The breakfast is a sensation in itself with a variety of hot and cold dishes served on

several trolleys. The star attraction is Marc Veyrat himself; a young chef always wearing his Savoyard mountain hat. This is not just a fad. Marc regularly goes up in to the mountains and collects alpine herbs to embellish and flavour his dishes. I have rarely eaten better as dish after dish was presented, starting with at least 10 different varieties of amuse bouche served on a piece of tree bark. Among Veyrat's specialities are sea urchin mousse with its juice and grilled red mullet with olive oil. Why not try the remarkable cheese trolley with an enormous choice. During the winter Marc Veyrat also runs an excellent restaurant in Megéve called Ferme de mon Père.

Les Baux-de-Provence

Oustaù de Baumanière ★★1/2

Tel: 04 90 54 33 07 Fax: 04 90 54 40 46
(Closed January & February)

When motoring through France this is one of the finest places to stop for dinner and an overnight stay. Our family have done this many times over the years en route to or from the Côte d'Azur. The setting is stunning as you come over the ridge and descend slowly into the valley of Les Baux. The Oustau is a 15th century farmhouse turned into a luxurious hotel with gardens, a swimming pool, and most importantly a two and a half star restaurant. The hotel was started by a Paris architect Raymond Thuilier, who became a top chef. I knew him well and enjoyed our meetings. He died a few years ago in his mid nineties and is succeeded by his grandson Jean-André Charial. After a dip in the pool, just in front of the restaurant, sit down and enjoy his cooking with dishes such as langoustine roasted with pistachios and lemon, truffle ravioli with leeks, lamb en croute and for dessert, crepe soufflé. There is a magnificent wine list but you can also choose reasonably priced Provençale wines.

Beaulieu-sur-Mer

La Réserve de Beaulieu ★★

5 bvd Maréchal Leclerc
Tel: 04 93 01 00 01 Fax: 04 93 01 28 99
(Closed for lunch June – September)

One of the oldest and most famous hotels on the Riviera is now again featuring some of the best cooking on the Côte under the guidance of Chef Christophe Cussac. You will dine on a beautiful open terrace just above the swimming

pool and the small harbour beyond. Expensive but worth it! Do try the Mediterranean sea bass known locally as loup cooked in local Provençale wine. Sommelier Jean-Louis Balla gives good advice on reasonably priced wines.

Cancale

Maison de Bricourt ★★★

Rue Duguesclin
Tel: 02 99 89 64 76 Fax: 02 99 89 88 47
(Closed mid-December to mid-March & Wednesday)
Wherever you travel in France there are good restaurants - cooking comes so naturally to the French - but in the north there are fewer in the top category. Maison de Bricourt is therefore a real find; it is attractively located on the coast overlooking the bay of Mont St Michel and also near the port of St Malo. Chef/patron Olivier Roellinger who was born in this 18th century farmhouse creates excellent seafood dishes, of course, such as lobster with herbs from the islands and sea bass and sole with different sauces and also langoustines. Among meat dishes there is a remarkable saddle of lamb and an excellent pigeon. Roellinger and his wife Jane also run an hotel and a bistro. His prices are among the lowest for a three star restaurant - the lunch menu is only FF320.

Cannes

Neat ★

11 square Mérimée
Tel: 04 93 99 29 19 Fax: 04 93 68 84 48
(Closed Sunday)
Richard Neat used to be the chef and co-owner of Pied a Terre in London but then he and his French wife Sophie decided to take off for the Côte d'Azur where he opened under his own name in Cannes right next to the Palais du Festival and the port. Neat has made a good start and on a first visit my wife and I enjoyed a brochette of scallops and filet of rabbit with olives. On the menu we also noticed a red mullet dish and oysters fried crisply over hollandaise sauce. There is also a menu for FF270 which is very reasonable in this part of the world. In good weather you can dine out at the terrace tables.

Chagny

Lameloise ★★★

Place d'Armes

Tel: 03 85 87 65 65 Fax: 03 85 87 03 57

(Closed Tuesday & Thursday lunch & Wednesday)

Should you happen to be driving on the autoroute du soleil from northern France to Provence and the Côte d'Azur - or vice versa - the perfect overnight stop is in the little town of Chagny in Burgundy, about half way. Lameloise is a good, but not luxurious, hotel but it has a three star restaurant under the direction of Jacques Lameloise. My wife and I have stayed and dined here many times and have always enjoyed a superb dinner. The hotel is in a 15th century house on a small town square, but still fairly quiet. The town is surrounded by famous Burgundy vineyards. Among the interesting culinary creations that I have enjoyed is a dish of three different foie gras - au naturel, with figs and with red wine. Another good creation is Burgundian snails with red butter and why not also try poached eggs with caviar on a bed of puréed potatoes with chives. To end the meal I enjoyed, on my last visit, gratin de pamplemousse à praline rose. Here you must of course drink Burgundy wines with your meal. Travel tips: coming from the north exit the motorway at Beaune; coming from the south you exit at Chalon-sur-Seaune.

Courchevel

Le Chalet de pierres FF

Courchevel 1850

Tel: 04 79 08 18 61 Fax: 04 79 08 38 06

(Only open December – April)

This is one of my son's favourite mountain restaurants in the Alps. Under the Verdons bubble car, around two-thirds of a kilometre above the village, lies one of the largest mountain chalet restaurants in France. A charming building with tables upstairs and downstairs and a terrace that seems to be able to seat a vast number of people. Yvette Saxe overseas a staff dressed splendidly in Savoyard mountain uniform and serves classical French cooking and all Savoyard dishes. Buy a ticket for the outstanding dessert table, where up to 25 cakes and puddings are produced daily; I particularly like the nut cake, covered in walnuts. In the evening if you reserve, you can be collected by snow-cat in the village and enjoy lamb smoked over the open fire.

Also recommended:

Bel Air FF

Courchevel 1650

Tel: 04 79 08 00 93

The best mountain eating in 1650. Very popular with the English. Excellent meat dishes.

Eugenie les Bains

Les Prés d'Eugénie ★★★

Tel: 05 58 05 06 07 Fax: 05 58 51 10 10

(Closed 3 weeks in December & January & February)

Do you want to become healthier and at the same time eat some very fine food? I am sure you do and I have the answer - you must visit Michel and Christine Guerard at Eugenie Les Bains, their health farm with a three star restaurant in South-West France. Guerard, generally considered to be one of the greatest chefs in France, is the creator of 'cuisine minceur', the slimming gourmet diet which made him famous years ago. If you stay a few days here you can enjoy the peace and comfort of the magnolia and verbena gardens and combine health treatments and a dip in the pool with some superb meals. On our last visit we, without question, became healthier by enjoying dishes such as morel mushrooms with asparagus, crayfish with herbs and grilled pigeon. You should also try the local wines. Service is outstanding.

Eze

Château de la Chèvre d'Or ★★

Rue Barri

Tel: 04 92 10 66 66 Fax: 04 93 41 06 72

(Closed November-March)

Perched like an eagles' nest 1300 feet above the sea with breathtaking views of the Mediterranean far below. The restaurant is part of a small 18th century hotel with a lovely little swimming pool. New chef Marc Delacourt has revitalised the cuisine and well deserves the 2 stars that he receives in this guide. In summertime you can enjoy a drink next to the pool with a beautiful view overlooking Cap Ferrat and the stunning coastline.

Grasse

Bastide Saint Antoine ★★1/2

48 avenue Henri Dunant

Tel: 04 93 70 94 94 Fax: 04 93 70 94 95

Summer dining is on a beautiful terrace overlooking a wide lawn. I have known Chef Jacques Chibois for many years and followed his progress from the coast up to this lovely hilltop mansion in the middle of an olive grove on the outskirts of Grasse. On a recent visit I enjoyed papillon de langoustine followed by filet of red mullet finishing with a millefeuille. In the evening you can dine in front of the fireplace. Don't miss it! Chibois certainly deserves his two and a half stars.

Illhaeusern

Auberge de l'Ill ★★★

Rue de Collonges

Tel: 03 89 71 89 00 Fax: 03 89 71 82 83

(Closed February, Monday and Tuesday)

If any restaurant is worth a special detour during a trip to France then this is it. As the French say: "Ca vaut le voyage!" The Auberge is on a small peaceful river, the Ill, and you can take your pre-meal glass of champagne at tables literally on the bank by the flowing water. In the restaurant most tables also overlook the river. The Auberge has been family-owned for a very long time but only reached greatness when Paul Haeberlin took over. He has been a three-star chef for a long time and during many visits over the years I have been able to vouch for his skill. His son Marc is now jointly in charge. Paul's brother Jean-Pierre runs the restaurant, is also a talented artist and once did a drawing of the restaurant for me. And what about the food, the wine, the service: all outstanding as you might expect. As we are in Alsace (south of Strasbourg, near Colmar) foie gras is the speciality and with that you must drink Alsace wines. The wine list is excellent and I recommend going local under the guidance of sommelier Serge Dubs, who is one of the best. Other suggestions: salmon soufflé, sturgeon filet with chou croutes and spit-roasted chicken from Bresse.

St Jean, Cap Ferrat

Le Sloop FF

Yacht harbour

Tel: 04 93 01 48 63 Fax: 04 93 01 48 63

(Closed Wednesday & mid November – mid December)

There are 15 or more restaurants in the attractive yacht harbour of St Jean. My favourite, and generally considered the best, is Le Sloop which also happens to be the favourite of Andrew Lloyd Webber. Last summer we enjoyed an excellent but inexpensive dinner there. While dining you can look at the many yachts moored just a few yards away. Try the tartare of salmon, flan de langouste or local fish dorade. Friendly welcome by Mme Therlicocq.

Juan les Pins

La Terrasse, Juana ★★

La Pinede, Avenue Georges Gallice

Tel: 04 93 61 08 70 Fax: 04 93 61 76 60

(Open April – October, Closed Monday & Wednesday lunch)

If you can manage a summer visit to Restaurant La Terrasse in Hotel Juana you might be lucky and catch the annual Jazz festival in Juan-Les-Pins, which is just sensational. On my last visit saxophone and trumpet sounds were just kicking in as I ordered my dessert. The Jazz bands perform by the beach, yards from La Terrasse. Chef Christian Morisset's cooking is superb. Try the scampi as a starter followed by lamb in Pauillac. It is the favourite Riviera hangout of famous American entertainer Bill Cosby whom I have had the pleasure of meeting there several times.

Joigny

Côte St Jacques ★★★

14 Faubourg de Paris

Tel: 03 86 62 09 70 Fax: 03 86 91 49 70

(Closed January)

The A6 motorway from Paris south is for obvious reasons known as the 'autoroute du soleil'. If you plan to travel south on it I can recommend the perfect place to stop for lunch - it is only 144 km (90 miles) south of Paris. The name is Côte St Jacques in Joigny - a high quality restaurant with rooms where I have stayed overnight several times and enjoyed the view over the river Yonne and made use of their swimming pool. I have also dined well there

thanks to chef Jean Michel Lorain who has taken over from his father Michel but it remains very much a family enterprise. I have particularly enjoyed grilled Brittany lobster with fresh morels and green asparagus, and turbot cooked in a salt crust ending with spiced honey cake with caramel ice-cream and salted butter.

Lorgues

Bruno ★1/2

Route de Vidauban
Tel: 04 94 85 93 93 Fax: 04 94 85 93 99
(Closed Sunday dinner & Monday September – June)
Clement Bruno is a gentle giant who loves black truffles more than most and serves them to his customers as often as possible. To reach Bruno and the truffles you have to leave the Provençale motorway at Arcs and drive a few kilometres north. It is not easy to find but well worth the effort as his truffle dishes are extremely tasty and very reasonably priced (menu FF300 at time of writing). I discovered Bruno by chance and have since made many return visits. The restaurant is peacefully located in a Provençale Mas surrounded by vineyards just before Lorgues. There are also four rooms if you wish to stay the night. In good weather meals are served on the terrace. Some of Bruno's favourite dishes that you can enjoy are scrambled eggs with truffles, ravioli with foie gras and white truffles from Italy, or, most special of all, an entire truffle baked in pastry. There are also many other tempting dishes!

Lyon

Paul Bocuse ★★★

Collonges-au-Mont-d'Or
Tel: 04 72 42 90 90 Fax: 04 72 27 85 87
The name Paul Bocuse is famous throughout the world of gastronomy. He comes from a long line of chefs, from father to son since 1765, all living in the same village on the banks of the river Saône, five kilometres north of Lyon. Michelin rewarded Paul Bocuse with three stars already in 1965 and he is now easily the longest holder of three Michelin stars in the world. The Florman Guide also awards Bocuse three stars. People come from all over the world to eat at Paul Bocuse. When I lived in Paris I would sometimes take the high speed TGV train on the two-hour trip to Lyon to lunch at Bocuse. President Giscard d'Estaing awarded Bocuse the Legion d'Honneur and invited him for lunch at the Elysée Palace in Paris. Bocuse accepted but asked to cook the lunch himself, with some

other famous chefs, and then created the truffle soup VGE, named after the President (Valerie Giscard d'Estaing). In the luxurious Bocuse dining room is an open fireplace where Bresse chicken, legs of lamb and other delicacies are roasting. If this does not tempt you why not try a famous fish dish which is sea bass en croute with sauce Choron. Every second year the most famous cookery competition for chefs from all over the world is organised by Bocuse in Lyon. It is called Bocuse d'Or. How can you not visit such a famous restaurant?

Léon de Lyon ★★

1 rue Pleney
Tel: 04 72 10 11 12 Fax: 04 72 10 11 13
(Closed Sunday and Monday & 3 weeks in July/August))
The Lyon area is the gastronomic heartland of France and although Paris has now attracted more starred restaurants Lyon and surroundings can boast some fine cuisine and just about the best produce. Sited on a peninsula between the rivers Rhône and Saône, Leon de Lyon has a fine city centre location. Chef Jean-Paul Lacombe and his wife Fabienne offer many traditional Lyonnais dishes such as the classic quenelles de brochet (pike) with sauce Nantua and chevreuil rôti sur l'os and l'epaule d'agneau braissée (braised shoulder of lamb).

Mionnay

Alain Chapel ★★★

Tel: 04 78 91 82 02 Fax: 04 78 91 82 37
(Closed January, Monday and Tuesday lunch)
When Alain Chapel was alive he was considered one of the three or four greatest French chefs of modern times. He was an inspiration to most of his colleagues and some of today's greatest chefs acknowledge their debt to him. I was privileged to meet him and sample his cuisine many times. Sadly he died too young, ten years ago, but Madame Suzanne Chapel and chef Philippe Jousse keep the standards high. Mionnay is a little bit off the beaten track north-east of Lyon and can best be reached by taking exit 3 from the motorway going round east of Lyon. There are some most attractive selections on the menu and let me mention dishes such as roasted langoustines with spices and lime butter and duckling from Challans au griottes (red cherries). There is a good value lunch menu for slightly over FF300.

Monte Carlo (+377)

Louis XV ★★★

Hôtel de Paris, Place Casino
Tel: 92 16 29 76 Fax: 92 16 69 21
(Closed Tuesday and Wednesday)

Alain Ducasse is probably the most talked-about star chef today. With restaurants in London, Paris and New York he is certainly spreading his wings but in Monte Carlo at the classic Hotel de Paris (facing the casino) he runs one of the most elegant restaurants in the world with the cuisine to match. The china and table settings are well suited to the wonderful Mediterranean cooking, among the very best. The menu features many Provençale dishes and in season the black truffle is prominent. The wine cellar contains some 250,000 bottles, giving you a vast choice.

Montpellier

Jardin de Sens ★★★

11 avenue St-Lazare
Tel: 04 99 58 38 38 Fax: 04 99 58 38 39
(Closed Monday & Wednesday lunch, Sunday & January)

Jacques and Laurent Pourcel are, I can safely say, the only twins who cook to three star standard. They certainly are very talented brothers and I very much enjoyed our last meal and stay there. The restaurant is part of a small modern hotel on a non-descript backstreet. However the rooms are very comfortable and there is a small swimming pool on the roof. The dining room looks like an amphitheatre and has a glass wall leading on to an attractive garden with fountains and ponds. As it is not far from the coast the cooking is full of Mediterranean flavours in dishes such as oursin (sea urchins), coquille St Jacques sautée and a brochette of gambas. The wine list offers many choices from the region - do try them.

Nice

La Chaumière FF

384 bvd de l'Observatiore, Les 4 Chemins, Grande Corniche
Tel: 04 93 01 77 68 Fax: 04 93 76 93 88
(Dinner only – closed Sunday)

Very few quality restaurants are not listed in any guide but here is an exception. La Chaumiere ('the cottage' in English) is unique. Located high above the sea and Cap Ferrat on the so-called Grand Corniche it has been well

known and appreciated on the Côte D'Azur for many years and offers it's customers the same menu year after year and back they come for more of the same. Their formula is to cook the entire meal in the open fire in front of you. The choice is limited to beef or lamb. To start with there are crudités, paté and other hors d'oeuvres to consume while you are watching your meat being roasted in front of you. The potatoes are baked in the ashes and the bread is lightly toasted, also on the open fire. This has been a Florman's favourite for many years and now, for the first time, it appears in a restaurant guide. Provençale wines are served in carafes - just choose red or white. Booking is essential.

Reims

Boyer Les Crayères ★★★

64 boulevard Vasnier
Tel: 03 26 82 80 80 Fax: 03 26 82 65 52
(Closed Monday, Tuesday lunch)

There are very few restaurants of top gastronomic status in the north of France but Boyer is the great exception. If you should happen to be travelling on the autoroute from the Channel south, Boyer is the perfect stopover, located on the outskirts of Reims, the capital of Champagne. It not only has marvellous food but also presents it in beautiful grounds with a very nice garden. The restaurant is in a 19th century chateau with 19 rooms right in the heart of the champagne district. Madame Elyane Boyer gives you a warm welcome while her husband Gérard prepares sumptuous dishes. I like it so much that not long ago I took a large group of friends from England to eat and stay here for the weekend. Recommended dishes are truffles en croute with sauce Perigueux, lobster from Brittany, grilled in its shell with sweet wine. Your first drink should of course be a glass of champagne and the wine list offers an extensive choice.

Roanne

Troisgros ★★★

Place Gare
Tel: 04 77 71 66 97 Fax: 04 77 70 39 77
(Closed Tuesday & Wednesday & 3 weeks in August)

Here is a classic three star restaurant, somewhat off the beaten track, but very much a destination for all true gastronomes. Roanne is about an hours' drive from Lyon and slightly less from the Paris-Lyon motorway. Troisgros is also a hotel and is located directly opposite the railway sta-

tion. The hotel has been upgraded and the modern rooms are very comfortable. Outside is a remarkable statue made of thousands of forks - quite a sight! The Troisgros family have been famous chefs for many years. Pierre Troisgros, and his son Michel, serve some of the best food in France and it is so popular that you are advised to book. On my visits - and there have been many - I try to look into the kitchen which is considered one of the best designed and equipped anywhere. Some of the dishes I have enjoyed are saumon a l'oseille (salmon poached in sorrel sauce) a dish created by Troisgros, ecrevisses (crayfish) au court bouillon and canette de Challans laquée (duckling from Challans) with soufflé potatoes - delicious.

Saulieu

Côte d'Or ★★★

2 rue Argentine
Tel: 03 80 90 53 53 Fax: 03 80 64 08 92
Roughly half way between Paris and Lyon, in the little town of Saulieu, Bernard Loiseau offers you a room, a garden and a three star restaurant with unusual modern food. It is a peaceful and rustic place and you can concentrate very much on sampling some unusual dishes. When my wife and I stayed there we enjoyed the classic dish La Poularde de Bresse à la vapeur 'Alexandre Dumaine' in two servings. Alexandre Dumaine was a world famous chef who ran the Côte d'Or in the 1950's & 60's. Loiseau is a bit controversial. Another famous chef (in a much talked about incident) looked at the river in front of his garden and said to some visitors: "what you see there running are the sauces of Bernard Loiseau". He has been praised and criticised for his minimalist sauces but he is still considered one of the most outstanding chefs in France.

Strasbourg

Buerehiesel ★★★

Parc de l'Orangerie
Tel: 03 88 45 56 65 Fax: 03 88 61 32 00
(Closed Tuesday, Wednesday & 3 weeks in August)
The Alsace region is renowned not only for it's unique wines but also for the high quality of many of the restaurants in the area. One of the best, possibly the best, is Buerehiesel, attractively located in a glass pavilion in the Parc de l'Orangerie, very near the European Council offices. Chef proprietor Antoine Westermann is one of the most gifted and respected chefs in France - a true three-

star chef. While looking out onto the park I have tried and enjoyed crayfish bisque and afterwards duck à l'orange, a great speciality. An excellent dessert is crushed strawberries with vanilla sorbet. Madame Vivienne Westermann is charming and the expert sommelier is Jean-Marc Zimmerman.

Also recommended:

Au Crocodile ★★★

10 rue Outre
Tel: 03 88 32 13 02 Fax: 03 88 75 72 01
Three star cooking by Emile Jung. Excellent wine cellar. Look for the crocodile near the entrance. Full review in next edition.

Tours

Jean Bardet ★★

57 rue Graison
Tel: 02 47 41 41 11 Fax: 02 47 51 68 72
(Closed Monday & Tuesday lunch)
If you want to sample the star cuisine of Jean Bardet I would recommend also staying overnight in their hotel, the Chateau Belmont, built of white Tourain stone, on the right bank of the river Loire, with large attractive rooms and a swimming pool in the garden. Madame Sophie Bardet will give you a warm welcome while her husband prepares some exquisite dishes for your meal. I can recommend bouillon crème au langoustines and a fricassée of asparagus with mushrooms. The desserts are special, for example hot sabayon à l'orange or a hot tarte aux pommes.

Valence

Pic ★★1/2

285 avenue Victor Hugo
Tel: 04 75 44 15 32 Fax: 04 75 40 96 03
(Closed Sunday dinner & Monday)
The late, great Jacques Pic made this a well-known and much-liked gourmet stop. Now his daughter Anne Pic has taken over the stoves while her husband, David Sinapian, runs the hotel and looks after the wine cellar. In summertime it is very pleasant to eat outdoors in the garden. The hotel has twelve reasonably priced bedrooms for the travelling gourmet. There is also a second, simpler bistro restaurant (Auberge du Pin) under the same management. I have enjoyed many meals at Pic and had the pleasure of meeting

Jacques several times. Here are a few suggestions: a fish dish I like is sea bass with caviar and also gratin d'ecrevisses (crayfish); an excellent meat dish is a thick cut côte d'agneau with mint.

Vézelay

L'Espérance ★★★

à St-Père

Tel: 03 86 33 39 10 Fax: 03 86 33 26 15

(Closed Tuesday & Wednesday lunch & February)

Marc Meneau's restaurant is to be found below the hill top village of Vezelay with its basilica. The restaurant is large with glass walls that open up to the attractive garden, where you can take your pre-meal aperitif. On my last visit I had a room in the hotel above the restaurant with a garden view. A visit here is never wasted and I consider Meneau a very fine chef, although the red guide has taken away one of his stars, while Gault Millau gives him their top rating of 19. There are some very tempting dishes on offer, for example langoustines en chaud-froid, poached duck foie gras and, to finish, banane tigrée with passion fruit. This is an excellent stopping-off place when motoring through France.

Vienne

Pyramide ★★★

14 boulevard Fernand Point

Tel: 04 74 53 01 96 Fax: 04 74 85 69 73

(Closed Tuesday, Wednesday & February)

For many years the greatest chef in France, and possibly the world, was Fernand Point, owner of Pyramide. He was called the 'chef of the century' and many of his pupils, including Paul Bocuse, went on to their own three star careers. Many famous people, such as the Aga Khan, the Duke of Windsor and so on, travelled to Vienne to eat 'Chez Point'. I consider myself fortunate to have done the same and enjoyed many a meal there with my family. We usually stayed overnight in the hotel, and breakfasted in the beautiful garden, on the way to the Côte d'Azur, and I would advise you to do the same. After a difficult period the Pyramide has now been back in top form for a few years and I am happy to award three stars to chef Patrick Henriroux. He serves many unusual dishes such as frogs legs with morels on an asparagus cream ravioli and omble chevalier, or pigeon breast with giblets. You can round this off with parfait de moines de Chartreuse.

Vonnas

Georges Blanc ★★★

Tel: 04 74 50 90 90 Fax: 04 74 50 08 80
(Closed Monday, Tuesday; Wednesday lunch & January)
The little town of Vonnas (2,400 inhabitants) lies a short hour north of Lyon and is completely dominated, in the best way, by the Blanc family. In addition to the famous three-starred restaurant with rooms, there is a separate small hotel and a pleasant bistro and also a boutique. Georges Blanc is one of France's greatest restaurants, attractively located on the small river Veyle and with a garden and swimming pool. Originally called La Mere Blanc when mother Blanc was in charge, Georges Blanc has now been a three star restaurant for over twenty years (which is difficult to believe when you meet Georges himself). Vonnas is right in the heart of the Bresse region which produces some of the finest produce in France such as poulet de Bresse and the cheese bleu de Bresse. Not surprisingly the menu has several dishes relating to the area. Some dishes I have enjoyed here are fondant de poulard de Bresse with foie gras and roast wing of pigeon served in a boullion, and crayfish tails façon royale.

Also recommended:

Bonnieux

Auberge de l'Aiguebrun FF

6km along the D36, turn left onto the D943
Tel: 04 90 04 47 00 Fax: 04 90 04 47 01
A charming auberge at the bottom of a secluded valley in the Luberon mountains; outstanding Provençale cooking.

Bordeaux

Le Chapon Fin ★

5 rue Montesquieu
Tel: 05 56 79 10 10 Fax: 05 56 79 09 10
A famous historic restaurant with interesting décor. Food standards can only just match one star. Great wine list with many famous Bordeaux vintages - naturally.

Gincla

Hostellerie du Grand Duc FF

Tel: 04 68 20 55 02 Fax: 04 68 20 61 22

In the foothills of the Pyrenees, a grand old house serving traditional food. Worth the glorious drive.

Laguiole

Michel Bras ★★★

Route de L'Aubrac

Tel: 05 65 51 18 20 Fax: 05 65 48 47 02

Michel Bras is one of the greatest chefs in France but his restaurant is not easily accessible in the mountains and is closed November - March. Full review next year.

Lourmarin

Le Moulin de Lourmarin ★★

Rue Temple

Tel: 04 90 68 06 69 Fax: 04 90 68 31 76

The best in Provençale cooking. Young chef Edouard Loubet welcomes you in his 18th century converted mill in the middle of the village. Full review next year.

Marseilles

Petit Nice ★★

Anse de Maldormé

Tel: 04 91 59 25 92 Fax: 04 91 59 28 08

The best in Marseilles. Two star cooking overlooking the Mediterranean. Also hotel with 16 rooms.

Megève

Ferme de mon Père ★★1/2

367 route Crêt

Tel: 04 50 21 01 01 Fax: 04 50 21 43 43

The great Marc Veyrat moves from Lake Annecy to Megève in the Alps, December through March. Top food.

Montreuil

Chateau de Montreuil ★

4 chaussée des Capucins

Tel: 03 21 81 53 04 Fax: 03 21 81 36 43

My favourite overnight stop between London and Paris. Christian and Lindsay Germain give a friendly welcome. Excellent food and the best breakfast I can remember.

Mougins

Moulin de Mougins ★

Avenue Notre-Dame-de-Vie
Tel: 04 93 75 78 24 Fax: 04 93 90 18 55
Renowned chef Roger Vergé still produces his famous cuisine du soleil in his old mill house and attractive garden. I very much enjoy his fleurs des courgettes and braised lobster.

St Omer

Cygne FF

8 rue Caventou
Tel: 03 21 98 20 52 Fax: 03 21 95 57 12
A charming little restaurant in the centre of St Omer.

St Paul de Vence

Colombe d'Or FF

Tel: 04 93 32 80 02 Fax: 04 93 32 77 78
Famous for its extraordinary collection of modern art, but also its magnificent terrace shaded by fig trees.

Val Thorens

Fitz Roy Hôtel FF

Tel: 04 79 00 04 78 Fax: 04 79 00 06 11
A skiers' paradise, particularly the extravagant buffet on the terrace: swap your ski boots for slippers, and find sea urchins flown in from the Mediterranean. Owned by the Loubet family (see Loumarin).

Germany (+49)

Berlin

Bamberger Reiter ★

Regensburger Strasse 7
Tel: 030 218 4282 Fax: 030 214 74799
(Dinner only - closed Sunday & Monday)

This is one of the leading restaurants in Berlin, near the zooological gardens. Chef Christoph Fischer took over from his famous predecessor Franz Raneburger a couple of years ago and has kept standards high. Fischer serves what might be called new German cuisine but with an international touch. The menu changes daily. Look out for roast quail with mushroom tartare and turbot with chicory or monkfish in filo pastry.

Rockendorf's ★1/2

Passauer Strasse 5
Tel: 030 21 99 21 70 Fax: 030 21 99 21 74
(Closed Sunday)

For many years Siegfried Rockendorf has been the best known and possibly the best chef in Berlin. Last year he moved his restaurant into the centre of the city which immediately improved the flow of customers. Now that Berlin is once again the capital of Germany this is a good place to be. Rockendorf's cooking is light and imaginative. One of the specialities is lobster with various flavourings. When crayfish are in season they are on the menu. Foie gras, hot or cold, is another dish worth trying. The wine list does of course have a good variety of German wines but also some excellent Bordeaux.

VAU ★

Jägerstrasse 54
Tel: 030 202 9730 Fax: 030 202 97311
(Closed Sunday)

It is only four years ago that VAU opened in the Mitte district near the pretty square of Gendarme Markt. It is already one of Berlin's premier restaurants with a stylish interior and modern art on the walls. Chef Kolja Kleeberg is talked about as one of the rising stars in Berlin. He offers such interesting dishes as smoked sturgeon with caviar, marinated octopus slices with olive bread and roast duck with fried cabbage and bacon. For dessert you could try peach tart with white chocolate ice cream.

Also recommended:

Lorenz Adlon ★1/2

Hotel Adlon, Unter den Linden 77
Tel: 030 22 61 19 60 Fax: 030 22 61 22 22

In Berlin's most famous hotel on its most famous street we find chef de cusine Karlheinz Hauser in charge of this newly restored luxury restaurant serving some of the best food in Berlin.

Aschau im Chiemgau

Heinz Winkler ★★★

Kirchplatz 1
Tel: 080 521 7990 Fax: 080 521 79966
(Closed Monday lunch)

If you travel 80 kms east / south east from Munich on motorway A8 you will reach one of Germany's finest restaurants under the management of master chef Heinz Winkler. He built his career in Munich but some years ago took over this attractive country inn. Some of the rooms have beautiful views over the foothills of the Alps so you can combine gastronomy with beautiful surroundings. The cooking is of a high standard and recently Winkler was awarded the gold medal of the International Academy of Gastronomy. I very much look forward to my next visit when I intend to try his filet of turbot with leeks and madeira sauce and perhaps saddle of rabbit with white truffle butter and pasta. For dessert I might try a raspberry gratin with almond cream.

Baiersbronn

Schwarzwaldstube ★★★

Hotel Traube Tonbach
Tel: 07442 49 26 65 Fax: 07442 49 26 92
(Closed Monday & Tuesday)

In the heart of the Black Forest (Schwarzwald) there is a youngish man busy at his stoves in the Hotel Traube Tonbach. He is Harold Wohlfart and many think he is the greatest chef in Germany today. Heiner Finkbeiner, the proprietor, whose family have owned the hotel for over 100 years had the foresight to see the need for a gastronomic restaurant in a hotel otherwise devoted to relaxation, swimming and other sports. When I visited I built up my appetite by trying out both the indoor and the outdoor pools. I then sat down to one of the best composed and

tastiest meals I have eaten. Dear reader, get in your car and drive up to Baiersbronn. Among the culinary creations I can mention are crayfish tails with green asparagus tips and coriander in tomato jelly, grilled dover sole with parsley and capers and glazed breast of Barbary duck with apple and ginger compote and truffle juice.

Bergisch Gladbach

Dieter Müller ★★★

Schlosshotel Lerbach, Lerbacher Weg
Tel: 022 02 2040 Fax: 022 02 204940
(Closed Sunday, Monday & 3 weeks in July/August)
May I try to steer my readers to this superb restaurant in a small modernised castle hotel, set in 69 acres of parkland, half an hour east of Cologne. A few years ago Dieter Müller arrived to take charge of the stoves. As a result this is one of the finest restaurants in Germany. The dining area is spacious and comfortable with large windows overlooking the castle grounds. When I settled down and examined the menu I chose saltim- bocca de lapereau et salade de fins haricots and crepinette de pigeon au sang avec tranches de boudin, asperges vertes et sauces aux truffes. It is good to see a young German chef reach the gastronomic heights. The hotel rooms are first class and there is a health centre to take away those kilos you have just put on!

Cologne

Börsen-Restaurant Maitre ★

Unter Sachsenhausen 10
Tel: 0221 13 30 21 Fax: 0221 13 30 40
(Closed Saturday lunch, Sunday & 4 weeks in July/August)
Stockbrokers and bankers are well served by this well-established restaurant in the heart of the stock exchange building right in central Cologne, with a restrained art deco interior. The cooking by chef Erhard Schäfer is more French than German. His classic dishes include turbot in a court bouillon with caviar, mousseline and sea-food ravioli or wild pigeon stuffed with foie gras and morels.

Le Moissonier ★

Krefelder Strasse 25
Tel: 0221 72 94 79 Fax: 0221 732 5461
(Closed Sunday, Monday & 3 weeks in July/August)
We may be in Germany but here is a very French bistro with a friendly, relaxed atmosphere, turn of the century décor, with Tiffany lamps and art nouveau paintings on the

walls. The owners, Vincent and Liliane Moissonier, are excellent hosts, personally overseeing the seating and the service. Chef Eric Menchon cooks dishes such as marinated duck fillets with sorrel leaves, noisette of lamb with coconut curry and he likes to combine exotic with rustic ingredients, like a date mousse with chocolate and peanut sauce.

Düsseldorf

Im Schiffchen ★★★

Kaiserwerther Markt 9
Tel: 0211 40 10 50 Fax: 0211 40 36 67
(Closed Sunday and Monday)

French chefs cook in many countries. Jean Claude Bourgheuil is the leading French chef in Germany. His restaurant, Im Schiffchen ('in the little ship') is in a northern suburb of Düsseldorf, nicely positioned in the market place, a few yards from the river Rhine. The three star restaurant is on the first floor while the ground floor is run as a separate and simpler restaurant under the name Aalschokker, both are under the direction of Jean Claude. When I was last there I took a walk along the Rhine, looking out over the wide river before going upstairs to enjoy my dinner.

Hummerstübchen ★★

Hotel Fischerhaus, Bonafatiustrasse 35
Tel: 0211 59 44 02 Fax: 0211 59 797 59
(Closed Sunday and Monday)

Near the river Rhine you will find this excellent restaurant devoted, as the name implies, to serving lobster and other shellfish. If you love lobster (hummer in German) as I do, then this is the place for you. You can order a four-course lobster menu consisting of four varieties of lobster dishes including an outstanding lobster bisque.

Frankfurt

Restaurant Français ★

Frankfurter Hof, Bethmannstrasse 33
Tel: 069 215 02 Fax: 069 21 59 00
(Closed Saturday lunch, Sunday & Monday)

Frankfurter Hof is the number one hotel in Frankfurt and has always been a meeting place for bankers and business people. There are two restaurants, the main one being restaurant Français, definitely worth its star. There is also

Oscar, a trendy bistro. Restaurant Français, with its plush interior with large mirrors and well-spaced tables, is just about the best place to eat in Frankfurt. New young chef Patrick Bittner was formerly chef du partic at three-star restaurant Dieter Müller and serves a lighter, more modern French cuisine than before. Sit back, and enjoy some interesting creations such as perch with two different rosemary sauces or a vanilla soufflé.

Erno's Bistro ★

Liebigstrasse 15

Tel: 069 72 19 97 Fax: 069 173 38 38

(Closed Saturday, Sunday & 3 weeks June/July)

Although Frankfurt is the financial capital of Germany and therfore a prosperous and important city, the choice of top restaurants is rather limited. Erno's bistro which is not really a bistro at all is one of the best and very much "in". The décor is rustic but the atmosphere is good and so is the service. The cooking is Alsatian and southern French with some quite interesting dishes such as quail with chanterelle mushrooms and foie gras. An unusual dish is swordfish on a fricassée of squid and peppers. Desserts are substantial - try crème brulée with bourbon-vanilla or pear tart. Excellent wine list.

Tiger Restaurant ★

Heiligkreuzgasse 20

Tel: 069 92 00 22 25 Fax: 069 92 00 22 17

(Closed Sunday & Monday)

New chef, but continued high standards - that is the story of the Tiger. Martin Göschel, 29, having trained and cooked in other first class restaurants is now in charge. On the menu: quails' egg soup with lemongrass, John Dory fish with Chinese noodles and coconut chilli sauce and for dessert vanilla crème brulée with almond biscuits. There is an extensive wine list and a good bar in this city centre restaurant which is open for dinner only.

Also recommended:

Schlosshotel ★1/2

Kronberg im Taunus

Tel: 06173 7 01 01 Fax: 06173 7 01 267

This elegant and luxurious castle hotel can be reached by car from Frankfurt in less than half an hour. It is surrounded by an attractive park and the restaurant serves first class food. The castle has a fine display of valuable antiques.

Hamburg

Landhaus Scherrer ★★

Elbchaussee 130
Tel: 040 880 1325 Fax: 040 880 6260
(Closed Sunday)

Landhaus means country inn. It was opened 25 years ago by Albert Scherrer and has become one of Hamburg's two best restaurants. Mr Scherrer's widow Emmi Scherrer and chef Heinz Wehmann continue to keep standards high here along the river Elbe. Among the dishes on offer you will find medallions of monkfish in a lobster sauce and filet of veal with mushrooms and a red wine sauce. A north German speciality is saddle of venison on a bed of cabbage with celery and glazed cherries. I always like a cold dessert soufflé and here they have semolina soufflé with marinated berries and nectarine ice-cream.

Le Canard ★★

Elbchaussee 139
Tel: 040 880 5057 Fax: 040 889 13259
(Closed Sunday)

This restaurant is at the top of Hamburg's culinary world and it is well situated too, in a very modern building right by the River Elbe with fine river views. Here chef Josef Viehauser will provide you with an excellent meal in comfortable surroundings. He has built a solid reputation for his new simplified cuisine with never more than 3 ingredients on the plate, with no over complicated presentation, using only the best fresh produce. Try monkfish bordelaise or fillet of Arctic char with a ginger sauce and a purée of white beans.

Fischereihafen FF

Große Elbstrasse 143
Tel: 040 38 1816 Fax: 040 389 3021

Translated into English the name of this friendly and lively restaurant is 'the fishing harbour'. Naturally fish in every shape and form is on the menu (no meat). The chef buys his seafood straight from the fishing vessels in the harbour so freshness of the produce is guaranteed. This place is a Hamburg classic, much liked by business men and politicians (including Helmut Kohl). I have eaten here many times and always enjoyed it. Among dishes that stay in my memory are smoked eel with scrambled eggs, halibut and turbot with various garnishes and the Hamburg speciality, plaice, known in German as scholle. A new feature is a small oyster bar, where you can enjoy a light lunch.

Jahreszeiten Grill FF

Hotel Vier Jahreszeiten, Neuer Jungfernstieg 9
Tel: 040 349 40 Fax: 040 349 42 600

The grill room of the Four Seasons hotel is one of three restaurants in this fabulous luxury hotel - one of Europe's best. The grill room is simpler and more relaxed than the main restaurant and I enjoy eating here. Typical grill dishes such as T-bone steak are well presented. The lobster is also good and you can choose your own accompaniment among the sauces and vegetables offered. There is a prize-worthy three course business lunch for 45 marks. Enjoy your meal and the view over the lake.

Munich

Gasthaus Glockenbach ★

Kapuzinerstrasse 29
Tel: 089 534 043 Fax: 089 534 043

Karl Ederer is the chef and owner of this restaurant in an old vaulted building, previously an inn, with wooden panelling and decorated with very modern art. Ederer is a former pupil of master chef Eckart Witzigmann, who thinks Ederer is one of the best. The menu is traditional (no lemon grass or other exotic ingredients!) with mainly freshwater fish from the region. A special first course I recommend is fresh forest mushroom, sautéed in olive oil with a spoon of veal juice - delicious. A good dessert is pear tart with rose-hip sauce. The recommendations from the very qualified sommelier, Oliver Müller, come straight from the heart. The location is quite central, close to the main railway station.

Käfer Schänke FF

Schumannstrasse 1
Tel: 089 416 8247 Fax: 089 416 8623
(Closed Sunday)

Popular, friendly and much liked by Munich people is one way to describe this restaurant. Proprieter Max Käfer knows how to please customers and as a result Käfer Schänke's three dining rooms are almost fully booked every day. Now a new and very capable chef Fritz Schilling has arrived and ensures higher cooking standards. My wife and I have enjoyed several happy evenings here. A magnificent gourmet food shop on the ground floor is part of the establishment so you can stock up with delicacies.

Tantris ★★1/2

Johann-Fichte-Strasse 7
Tel: 089 361 9590 Fax: 089 361 8469
(Closed Sunday and Monday)

Most gourmet restaurants have a conventional or traditional décor but Tantris is different. It has a most unusual and very modern interior that does not appeal to everybody. It is however the best restaurant in Munich offering top class food, so do eat here if you are visiting this appealing city. Chef Hans Haas has established a high reputation and is well worth his two and a half stars. Perch-pike filets are cooked in a mustard crust with a purée of turnips, langoustine cooked in a curry and saffron sauce. A perfect dessert would be fried banana with a chocolate foam. The sommelier, Paula Bosch, one of the few lady sommeliers, will find the best wine to accompany your meal.

Also recommended:

Mark's Restaurant O

Mandarin Oriental, City Neuturmstrasse 1
Tel: 089 29 09 80 Fax: 089 22 25 39

The luxurious Hotel Rafael has recently become the even more luxurious Mandarin Oriental. Young chef Holger Stromberg creates ever more interesting dishes. Excellent wine cellar.

Stuttgart

Zirbelstube ★

Hotel Am Schlossgarten, Schillerstrasse 23
Tel: 0711 202 6808 Fax: 0711 202 6888
(Closed Sunday & Monday)

The Stube is one of the best and most elegant restaurants in Stuttgart. It is well located on the top floor of this first class hotel in the city centre, and next to the Schlossgarten Park. Chef Andreas Goldbach has created some tempting dishes and I suggest that you try stuffed artichokes with crayfish ragout or breast of pigeon with mushrooms. Sommelier Irene Kunert is in charge of an excellent wine cellar and you can confidently discuss your choice with her.

Speisemesterei ★★

Am Schloss Hohenheim
Tel: 0711 456 0037 Fax: 0711 456 0038
(Closed Sunday dinner, Monday & 3 weeks in July/August)
The name of this restaurant translates loosely into 'master cooking' and it is an apt description of the two-star quality of the cuisine. The restaurant is situated in a pavilion that is part of the former summer residence of the Duke of Würtemburg. It opened as a restaurant in 1993 with Martin Öxle as chef. Some of the specialities that are to be found on the menu are beetroot jelly with tartare, quails' eggs and caviar, a lovely starter. A good fish dish is John Dory in a pastry crust with stuffed flowers of courgettes. Good cheese trolley. Note: credit cards not accepted.

Wittlich

Waldhotel Sonnora ★★★

Auf dem Eichelfeld, Dreis
Tel: 06578 982 20 Fax: 06578 1402
(Closed Monday, Tuesday & January)
Wittlich is a small town in the Rheinland, between Koblenz and Trier, close to Luxembourg. The Sonnora is the newest three star restaurant in Germany and well worth the detour, if you are travelling in the area. The restaurant has recently been beautifully re-decorated. You can have drinks on the terrace or in the conservatory overlooking the gardens. The establishment is run by the Thieltges family with all members of the family involved. Chef Helmut Thieltges is in charge of the kitchen. His cooking is superb and his egg dishes are particularly memorable: poached eggs with Perigord truffles or scrambled eggs with caviar and cream of carrots or you could try his warm lobster medallions with scallops, served with gaspacho jelly - delicious. The wine list is very strong on Rhine wine from the region.

Great Britain (+44)

London

Aubergine ★

11 Park Walk SW10
Tel: 020 7352 3449 Fax: 020 7351 1770
(Closed Saturday lunch & Sunday)

In residential Chelsea the Aubergine is perhaps the best and well worth its star. Chef William Drabble presents an excellent French inspired menu in the comfortable dining room. I prefer the tables as far from the entrance as possible. During the winter season Aubergine offers a spectacular eight course truffle menu which is very interesting and unusual but quite expensive. Some dishes, which I have enjoyed, are scallops with a pea purée and red mullet with a tomato confit. The wine list is mainly French with good Bordeaux and Burgundy.

The Cadogan ★

75 Sloane Street SW1
Tel: 020 7235 7141 Fax: 020 7245 0994
(Closed Saturday lunch)

The Cadogan is well placed halfway down Sloane Street on the corner of Pont Street. It is an excellent hotel with its attractive Victorian and early Edwardian décor. It is famous for having had Oscar Wilde as a customer - indeed he was arrested in room 118. The restaurant is quiet and comfortable with a high standard of cooking by chef Graham Thompson. He is very talented and definitely deserves a star. He is one of my favourite chefs and I often go to the kitchen and get Graham's advice before ordering. Among his dishes are baked sea bass with barigoule artichoke and roast fillets of pigeon with celeriac purée and girolles.

The Capital ★★

22-24 Basil Street SW3
Tel: 020 7589 5171 Fax: 020 7225 0011

Eric de Chavot is one of the finest French chefs now working in London. In the Capital he has really found success with a menu of classic French dishes. On a recent visit I ordered the five-course tasting menu and started with nicely roasted scallops followed by boudin of foie gras. I could also have started with tuna carpaccio or pan-fried salmon with choucroute. Among main courses there is roast pigeon with lentils or gigot of rabbit with a black olive farcé. Our

dessert was thinly sliced strawberries on a biscuit pastry. The wine list is excellent but rather expensive with mainly French wines. The Capital hotel is one of the best small hotels in London, conveniently placed next door to Harrods. The restaurant with its understated elegance has been designed by David Linley, the son of Princess Margaret. The tables are well spaced, giving you privacy, and the service is very professional.

cheznico ★★1/2

Grosvenor House, 90 Park Lane W1
Tel: 020 7409 1290 Fax: 020 7355 4877
(Closed Saturday lunch & Sunday)

Nico Ladenis has gone low-key, both in name and prices. In 1999 he was still a rare three star chef in the Michelin guide but now he has opted not to be included. This does not mean that he has lost his talent. It is a very fine restaurant but with more simplified cooking and, bravo, lower prices. I have known and admired Nico for 20 years and I even chose his restaurant for my wedding lunch, which Nico cooked. Nico can be temperamental but he's a great chef and I urge my readers to venture forth and sample his cuisine. Discuss your selection of dishes with Dinah-Jane Ladenis or restaurant manager Jean-Luc Giquel.

Club Gascon ★

57 West Smithfield EC1
Tel: 020 7796 0600 Fax: 020 7796 0601
(Closed Saturday lunch & Sunday)

Foie gras in many shapes and forms is the speciality of this fairly simple and very French restaurant near London's business district. The proprietors Vincent Labeyrie and Pascal Aussignec (head chef) and most of the staff are French. As the name Gascon implies the menu is influenced by south-west France and there are also many wines from that area. When my wife and I lunched there recently we enjoyed the opportunity to order a number of small tasting-size dishes. We chose half a dozen and had them served two at a time. You can also order a glass of different wine to go with each course. Booking is absolutely essential.

The Connaught ★★

Carlos Place W1
Tel: 020 7499 7070 Fax: 020 7495 3262

There is no hotel I like more in London, and so do the many Americans who are always trying to book a room here. It is elegant, classic and conservative. There is also no

chef I like more than Michel Bourdin, a true French gentleman who has been the executive chef at the Connaught for twenty-six years. He also happens to be the favourite chef of the Queen Mother. Both she and Queen Elizabeth have visited Michel in his kitchen. Michel Bourdin is a recognised expert in truffles and to experience his truffle menu where every one of the five courses, including the cheese and the dessert, contain truffles is great. But beware the truffle season is short: December to April. Michel is planning to retire at the end of this year. His successor is young Frenchman Jerome Ponchelle. He is very talented so will keep standards high.

1837 ★1/2

Brown's Hotel, Albermarle Street W1
Tel: 020 7408 1837 Fax: 020 7493 9381
(Closed Saturday lunch & Sunday)

Brown's is the oldest hotel in London, opened in 1837. It is very well run by General Manager Peter Richards and the dining room has become one of the best in London, with food prepared by executive chef Andrew Turner, formerly with Albert Roux. I have a very high opinion of Andrew and recently organised a meal for friends here, where we took Andrew's special 'grazing' menu. This offers you the experience of having up to seven small dishes and with a different glass of wine chosen to suit each dish. We started with velouté of French rabbit with truffles and went on to seared foie gras with a coulis of green apple. We also had sea scallops and sweetbread - a superb dinner. We ended with warm creole bananas and coconut ice-cream with which we drank sweet Rivesaltes wine.

Floriana ★

15 Beauchamp Place SW3
Tel: 020 7838 1500 Fax: 020 7584 1464
(Closed Sunday & Monday lunch)

There are several good reasons for lunching or dining at Floriana. First there is the food which is classic Italian. Then there is the location - in fashionable Beauchamp Place - and then the attractive dining room, in cream and brown with a glass ceiling. Floriana is a creation of Riccardo Mazzucchelli whose aim it is to serve the best Italian food in London. As there was a change of head chef a few months ago it cannot yet be said how close he is to achieving this.

Foliage

★1/2

Mandarin Oriental Hyde Park
66 Knightsbridge SW1
Tel: 020 7235 2000 Fax: 020 7235 4552
(Closed Saturday lunch & Sunday)

This used to be the good old Hyde Park Hotel, a very traditional English hotel, where I used to drop in for a snack now and then. Now it has been taken over by the Mandarin Oriental Group and part of the large dining room has been turned into the Foliage restaurant overlooking Hyde Park. Presentation is important here with four types of wineglass and several tiny tasters. Executive chef David Nicholls, who I know from when he was at the Ritz, has really hit his stride here and this is now one of London's best hotel-restaurants. On my first visit I started with Scottish lobster with vinaigrette of crab, confit tomatoes and caviar dressing. My wife had ravioli of scallops with caramelised cauliflower.

Le Gavroche

★★★

43 Upper Brook Street W1
Tel: 020 7408 0881 Fax: 020 7409 0939
(Closed Saturday & Sunday)

For many years this has been one of my absolute favourites. Albert Roux, the French masterchef who created Le Gavroche has been a very good friend of mine for 20 years. His son Michel jr. took over a few years ago and has proved that he is also a great chef. Le Gavroche is really the complete restaurant; comfortable, elegant and with almost perfect service. Michel's skill at the stoves is matched in the dining room by restaurant manager Silvano Giraldin, generally considered to be the very best. He is assisted by headwaiter Jean-Claude Pechaut and head sommelier Thierry Tommasin who will pick the right wine to match your food and not necessarily a very expensive one (one of the talents of a good sommelier is to propose reasonably priced wines when requested). Delicious food and outstanding service does not come cheap of course but at lunch there is a good value menu for £40 which includes a half bottle of wine per person. I have several favourite dishes at Le Gavroche; here for example is a menu I chose when I lunched there recently with a group of friends: coeur d'artichaut "Lucullus", rouget sur risotto de coques et jus safrané, then filet de chevreuil a la sauce poivrade et airelles followed by délice glacé au tokaji aszu. A lovely dish, which I have also enjoyed, is soufflé Suisesse which is a Roux version of a cheese soufflé.

Gordon Ramsay ★★★

68-69 Royal Hospital Road SW3
Tel: 020 7352 4441 Fax: 020 7352 3334
(Closed Saturday & Sunday)

If you find yourself walking down Royal Hospital Road in Chelsea one day you might be surprised to find out that behind the discreet brown door at number 68 one of the greatest chefs cooking in Britain today is busy preparing some very delicate and original dishes. He is Gordon Ramsay, a Scottish ex-footballer (Glasgow Rangers) who is as dynamic and proficient in the kitchen as he was on the pitch. Gordon is a perfectionist who turns out some of the finest food in England. The restaurant is fairly small, nicely decorated with engraved glass walls , seating only 46. Ramsay's reputation is so high that you have to book at least a month ahead but do try. The dining room is run by Jean-Claude Breton, one of the best restaurant managers; the Sommelier is Ronan Sayburn. Among dishes you mustn't miss are oven-roasted tranche of foie gras with caramelised endives, Banyuls sauce, sweet and sour cherries; panaché of roasted sea scallops with a truffle-scented cauliflower purée and beignets with Barolo vinaigrette or fillets of red mullet cooked with saffron on a bed of marinated peppers and crab couscous with lemon and lime confit. Considering the high standard the set three-course lunch for £35 is good value.

John Burton-Race ★★

The Landmark, 222 Marylebone Road NW1
Tel: 020 7723 7800 Fax: 020 7723 4700
(Closed Saturday lunch & Sunday dinner)

For many years John Burton-Race owned and ran a very good country restaurant but now he has been tempted to London and has established himself in a large hotel - never an easy move, but happening more and more. The Landmark is a stylish hotel with a remarkable high atrium lobby. It is located away from the centre in Marylebone, opposite the station. Burton-Race's food has to be really excellent to attract enough customers out of the West End to fill the large dining room where he now is - and it is superb. John is now, in my opinion, one of the top ten chefs in Britain. When I dined there with some friends not long ago we had the following tasting menu: tomato consommé scented with coriander, crayfish tails roasted and flamed in cognac and corn-fed squab pigeon roasted with honey. The wines are mainly French. To counteract the high prices there are set menus for both lunch and dinner at £29.50 and £48.00 respectively.

Lundum's

FF

119 Old Brompton Road SW7
Tel: 020 7373 7774 Fax: 020 7373 4472
(Closed Sunday dinner)

London's only Danish restaurant is a good exponent of all that is best with Danish produce and Danish cooking. So what comes from Denmark? Fish and shellfish of course: the herring platter is a good example. Here you get marinated, spicy, curried and dill herrings. Then we come to the salmon family; you can have the salmon gravad (marinated) or smoked or salted or raw as a tartare. You can also have a selection as a mixed platter. Among fish dishes are pan-fried plaice with cranberries, grilled sea bass and oven-baked monkfish. Pork fillets in a prune and armagnac sauce is a meat dish I have enjoyed before going on to a crème brulée or Lundum's chocolate mousse. The entire Lundum family headed by Kay Lundum, his wife Connie and their son and daughter make this very much a family enterprise. It is a small but comfortable place, easily reached in South Kensington. My wife and I sometimes go there on Sundays for their brunch buffet for the very reasonable price of £15.50.

L'Oranger

★

5 St James's Street SW1
Tel: 020 7839 3774 Fax: 020 7839 4330
(Closed Saturday lunch & Sunday)

St James's is a popular area for luxury shopping. After shopping where better to stop in for lunch or dinner than L'Oranger, an attractive and elegant restaurant with good food and excellent service. Chef Kemal Benamar offers mainly French cuisine but also dishes such as salted cod and potato tartelette with shallots; canon of lamb with braised fennel. When I dined there I finished with a hazelnut soufflé with chocolate sauce and praline ice cream.

Orrery

★1/2

55 Marylebone High Street W1
Tel: 020 7616 8000 Fax: 020 7616 8080

The Conran group consists of some 16 restaurants of varying size and quality. The star performer is Orrery, which is certainly the best. Chef Chris Galvin is obviously given a free hand to produce dishes of a high standard. The first floor dining room sits atop the Conran shop in Marylebone. It is attractive with many mirrors, but extremely noisy - the acoustics are bad. When I lunched there not long ago my guest and I managed to move to a corner

table where we took the set lunch at £23.50 which is good value. There is also a menu gourmand of six courses for £45 which includes such tempting dishes as ballotine of foie gras, green pepper corns with balsamic jelly and seared sea scallops with a sauce nero. You can have the same menu with a different glass of wine for each course for £75.

Pétrus ★★

33 St James's Street SW1
Tel: 020 7930 4272 Fax: 020 7930 9702
(Closed Saturday lunch & Sunday)

Marcus Wareing is a very talented chef who has worked with the great Gordon Ramsay. He has now established his own distinct profile and last year Petrus was voted restaurant of the year by the respected Square Meal guide. The Michelin Red Guide gives Pétrus one star but I have decided to go ahead and give Wareing his second star already now. Pétrus is small and elegant and well located in exclusive St James's Street. It is now in the top group of London's gastronomic venues. Prices are fairly high but there are two set lunch menus for £26. Book well ahead, as tables are much in demand.

Pied à Terre ★1/2

34 Charlotte Street W1
Tel: 020 7636 1178 Fax: 020 7916 1171
(Closed Saturday lunch & Sunday)

Charlotte Street, just north of Oxford Street, is a popular street with many restaurants but Pied à Terre ranks as the best. A fairly small (40 seats) modern place with striking paintings, it has gone through some ups and downs but new chef, Australian Shane Osborn, is now firmly established as a one star plus chef, so I award him one and a half stars. Owner / manager David Moore is very hands on and personally buys the wine and compiles the wine list which has good choices, both from France and the new world, especially Australia. Osborn's cooking is of such high standard that I would recommend trying the tasting menu - either seven courses for £60 or nine (!) courses for £70. If this is too much, take the lunch menu, three courses for £23. I have eaten here many times and always enjoyed my meals.

Pomegranates

FF

94 Grosvenor Road SW1
Tel: 020 7828 6560 Fax: 020 7828 2037
Down by the river in a comfortable basement restaurant, Patrick Gwynn-Jones is the host and the creator of many interesting dishes. This restaurant has for many years been one of my favourites in London. I usually start with gravad lax (marinated salmon) with good spices and a lot of dill - perhaps the best in London. I then tend to order the Scottish fillet of beef, rare of course, which is also one of the best. The cuisine is eclectic, with many dishes brought back by Patrick from his travels abroad - for example Mauritian soup and West Indian curried goat. There is a small private dining room where groups of 6-10 dine at the large round table. Sometimes the atmosphere is more like a club with many regular customers dropping in. There is a very reasonably priced menu.

Roussillon

★

16 St Barnabas Street SW1
Tel: 020 7730 5550 Fax: 020 7824 8617
(Closed Saturday lunch & Sunday)
This is a hidden gem that deserves to be better known. Although it fills up in the evening at lunch-time it is a calm neighbourhood place in this Pimlico backwater. Young chef Alexis Gauthier is gaining a good reputation for his cooking and I feel confident that he deserves the star that I am giving him after my last two visits. In most restaurants vegetarians are rather neglected but here Gauthier offers a special 'garden menu' of soups, eggs and vegetables to please the growing minority of non meat eaters. Other dishes to mention are: wild sea bass on its crunchy skin with pea shoots, baby squid and black ink sauce, or grilled pigeon with fondant potatoes and button onions with pink liver. The wine list is French dominated and offers 25 wines by the glass many from Southern France.

The Square

★★

6-10 Bruton Street W1
Tel: 020 7495 7100 Fax: 020 7495 7150
(Closed Saturday lunch & Sunday)
How about having your meal prepared by a marathon runner? And a very good one too - both the runner and the meal. The runner is Philip Howard, chef and co-proprietor of this first class restaurant perfectly located in the heart of Mayfair. The Square offers modern French cooking in quality surroundings with well-spaced tables. Manager

Jacques Carlino ensures good attentive service and sommmelier Marc Moignoux can offer you a large selection of wines, particularly strong in Bordeaux and Burgundy. Here are a few dishes to consider from the current menu: start with velouté of globe artichokes with chanterelles and a soft poached truffled egg and move on to roast loin of venison with caramelised root vegetables, glazed pear and a celeriac cream. For dessert why not try soup of fruit with passion fruit jellies and coconut. There is a lunch menu for £25 which I had on my last visit.

La Tante Claire ★★★

Wilton Place SW1
Tel: 020 7823 2003 Fax: 020 7823 2001
(Closed Saturday lunch & Sunday)

Pierre Koffmann, chef patron, is a modest, almost shy, Frenchman from Gascony, who stays in the kitchen preparing his superb dishes rather than come out to greet the customers. He came to England exactly 30 years ago to work for the Roux brothers in Le Gavroche. He later became the first chef at the Waterside Inn before opening his own place, Tante Claire. A few years ago it transferred to the Berkeley Hotel giving Koffmann the challenge of twice as many mouths to feed. Pierre is famous for his signature dish, which is stuffed pig's trotters with morels. When you visit why not start with scallops, for example, or a superb crayfish bisque and then go on to the famous trotters. An interesting dessert is pistachio soufflé. The wine list is impressive and there are many reasonably priced regional French wines. The service is extremely good thanks to manager Christian Drean and his staff. There is a good value set priced lunch for £29. Tante Claire remains one of my favourites and I think it is a must for visitors to London looking for the very best.

Also recommended:

Bibendum ★

Michelin House, 81 Fulham Road SW3
Tel: 020 7581 5817 Fax: 020 7823 7925

A good place to entertain. A very attractive dining room at the top of the old Michelin building. The best oyster bar in London downstairs with ceramic wall tiles on motoring history.

Chez Bruce ★

2 Bellevue Road SW17
Tel: 020 8672 0114 Fax: 020 8767 6648

A bit difficult to reach but well worth the effort to sample

modern British cooking by Bruce Poole. Try stuffed saddle of rabbit. There are 20 wines by the glass and half-bottle.

Garbo's FF

42 Crawford Street, W1
Tel & Fax: 020 7262 6582
Owner and chef Ake Lindholm serves good, simple Swedish food. His great speciality is freshwater crayfish cooked in the traditional Swedish style with beer, dill and sea salt.

Mirabelle ★

56 Curzon Street W1
Tel: 020 7499 4636 Fax: 020 7499 5449
Under the supervision of proprietor Marco Pierre White new chef Martin Caws and general manager Christophe Capron run a very good restaurant with excellent food and service.

Nobu ★

19 Old Park Lane W1
Tel: 020 7447 4747 Fax: 020 7447 4749
Fashionable people eating top quality Japanese food in a very expensive, minimalist décor establishment.

Putney Bridge ★

1 Embankment, Lower Richmond Road SW15
Tel: 020 8780 1811 Fax: 020 8780 1211
Go down King's Road, cross Putney Bridge, and there on your right is a spectacular glass house with a fine restaurant.

Zafferano ★1/2

15 Lowndes Street SW1
Tel: 020 7235 5800 Fax: 020 7235 1971
Giorgio Locatelli's very popular Italian restaurant is always fully booked and with good reason as the cooking, by chef Andrew Needham, is of high standard and service is very good.

Incognico FF

117 Shaftesbury Avenue, WC2
Tel: 020 7836 8866 Fax: 020 7240 9525
Nico Ladenis's newest venture, managed by his daughter, Natasha. As it is right in the middle of theatreland it is an ideal place for after-theatre suppers. Good value for money.

Bath

Lettonie ★★

35 Kelston Road, Bath, Somerset
Tel: 01225 446 676 Fax: 01225 447 541
(Closed Sunday & Monday)

Lettonie is the French name for the Baltic state of Latvia. Why name a restaurant after a far away state? Because chef / patron Martin Blunos' parents came from Latvia and he respects French cuisine. He and his wife Siân have created an excellent restaurant with rooms on the outskirts of Bath. There are only four rooms (so book ahead) but they are very comfortable and overlook the garden and the valley beyond. When my wife and I dined there we stayed overnight and were able to enjoy a very good breakfast the next morning. The food well deserves the two stars I am awarding and so does the service, under the direction of manager Andrew Proctor. Starters I recommend are mussel and saffron cream soup 'en croute' or crab ravioli with a cognac cream sauce and shellfish oil. For the main course why not try seared beef fillet with grapes and slow cooked ox cheek in a red wine sauce and for a dessert hot rhubarb soufflé with a rhubarb and cardamom sauce and vanilla ice cream.

Blackburn

Northcote Manor ★1/2

Northcote Road, Langho, Lancashire
Tel: 01254 240 555 Fax: 01254 246 568
(Closed Saturday lunch)

Nigel Haworth and Craig Bancroft make a good partnership up in Lancashire. Northcote Manor is a first class country house hotel with a star restaurant, a few miles outside Blackburn. Nigel is a very innovative chef who well deserves his star. He likes to use Lancashire ingredients and is a chef with a 'terroir' reputation. He won the Egon Ronay Guides Chef of the Year award a few years ago. Let us look at some of his dishes, several of which I have sampled when staying at the manor. There are, for example, on the winter menu starters such as risotto of peeled prawns and basil, tortellini of salmon and crab and Mrs Kirkham's Lancashire cheese soufflé. A good main course is crusted rack of Pendle lamb and to mention a dessert, why not try iced apple crumble parfait. Craig Bancroft runs the hotel and dining room but his passion is the wine cellar, which has more than 400 bins with a selection from many countries.

Bray-on-Thames

The Fat Duck ★★1/2

High Street, Bray-On-Thames, Berkshire
Tel: 01628 580 333 Fax: 01628 776 188
(Closed Sunday dinner & Monday)

Do you want to eat an interesting high quality meal presented in a totally different way? If so take yourself to Bray - 45 minutes from London on the M4 (exit 8/9). In a rustic dining room in a simple white building on the main street that gives no hint of what is to come, you will be presented with taste combinations that you have never experienced before. Heston Blumenthal is a tremendously innovative chef who through combining the most unusual ingredients presents small dishes in amuse-bouche fashion. When I lunched there with a group of friends we were given nine miniature courses, with such delights as crab biscuit with roast foie gras, crystallised seaweed, marinated salmon with oyster vinaigrette, and saddle of lamb cooked at a low temperature with a garlic and coffee dentelle and onion purée. Heston is constantly experimenting with new ideas so I strongly recommend a visit.

Waterside Inn ★★★

Ferry Road, Bray-on-Thames, Berkshire
Tel:01628 620 691 Fax: 01628 784 710
(Closed Monday, Tuesday & January)

The name Roux is synonymous with high quality cooking in Britain. While elder brother Albert has been the patron of Le Gavroche since the start, younger brother Michel has made the Waterside Inn on the banks of the Thames his domain. He and his Australian born wife Robyn are very good hosts in their delightful white painted restaurant where the wide bay windows give a fine view of the river. In good weather you can take both your aperitif and later your digestif on the terrace. The dining room is supervised by restaurant director Diego Masciaga, one of the finest professionals in the country. He and his staff are most attentive. And what about the food? Well, it is really at the top of the gastronomic pyramid, featuring dishes such as quenelle de brochet à la lyonnaise and selle d'agneau farcie aux champignons sauvages, legumes d'hiver rôtis et jus au thym. I have been fortunate to have had many fine meals here over the years. Michel Roux is a "Meilleur Ouvrier de France" in pastry. This is a rare distinction and he is the only holder of this title in Britain.

Chagford

Gidleigh Park ★★

Chagford, Devon

Tel: 01647 432367 Fax: 01647 432574

If you are travelling down to Devon in the West Country and feel like staying in a beautiful timbered country house hotel with the best food in the region do head for Gidleigh Park. It is set in a lovely isolated spot with a beautiful approach road and a small river just below the hotel. Paul and Kay Henderson have now been running this charming, friendly and sophisticated hotel for over twenty years. Try chef Michael Caines' Jerusalem artichoke and truffle soup followed by roast pigeon on a potato galette with pan-fried foie gras and Madeira sauce. There is an award-winning wine list.

Cheltenham

Le Champignon Sauvage ★★

24-26 Suffolk Road, Cheltenham, Gloucestershire

Tel: 01242 573 449 Fax: 01242 254 365

(Closed Sunday, Monday & 3 weeks in June)

There are not many restaurants in England worthy of two Florman stars. Le Champignon Sauvage (wild mushroom) is one of the smallest, and least publicised of this group. Discreetly located on a non-descript street in south Cheltenham it does offer a warm and friendly welcome by Helen Everitt-Matthias and her husband David, the chef. After a welcoming drink in the small bar you take your seat in the blue and yellow dining room with modern art on the walls. The food that awaits you is best described as modern European and is good value. Dishes to try are caille rôtie, crème de carottes à la cardamome and filet de barbue, sauté de poire et céleri-rave, jus d'orge brulé. For dessert I particularly enjoyed feullantine de mangue 'Thai' with sirop de vin rouge.

Longridge

Paul Heathcote's ★1/2

104-106 Higher Road, Longridge, Lancashire

Tel: 01772 784 969 Fax: 01772 785 713

(Closed Saturday lunch, Monday & Tuesday)

Lancashire is not exactly buzzing with restaurants serving really fine food but here is a star performer. Paul Heathcote, born and bred in Lancashire, had early ambitions to be a successful chef. After many setbacks he trai-

ned with Michel Bourdin at the Connaught and Raymond Blanc in Oxford. He opened his own restaurant in 1990 and it is now the most famous in the area. He also has two brasseries called Simply Heathcotes. At his main restaurant there are ample opportunities to try out Paul's many exciting dishes. In addition to a la carte and the 5 course menu there is a 10 course menu de degustation. I particularly enjoyed the roasted squab pigeon - a dish not always appreciated in England but much loved in France. To end the meal I did of course order black pudding.

New Milton

Chewton Glen ★

Christchurch Road, New Milton, Hampshire
Tel: 01425 275 341 Fax: 01425 272 310
Owners Martin and Brigitte Skan have devoted many years to making Chewton Glen one of the finest country house hotels in the world, and with a restaurant to match. On the edge of the New Forest near the south coast Chewton Glen is well situated for a weekend or short holiday. The gardens, the two swimming pools, the gymnasium and sauna, the golf course and the tennis courts will all help to build your appetite for the first class dinner that follows. There are two dining rooms, the Marryat and the Conservatory and they both offer well-composed dishes by chef Pierre Chevillard. We enjoyed langoustines with paprika and tarragon mayonnaise followed by filet of lamb with a crust of mustard and herbs. The sommelier Mark Walton has an extensive wine list.

Oxford

Le Manoir aux Quat' Saisons ★★1/2

Church Road, Great Milton, Oxfordshire
Tel: 01844 278 881 Fax: 01844 278 847
If you wish to enjoy a gastronomic meal outside London one of the best addresses is Le Manoir aux Quat' Saisons, an hour's drive towards Oxford. There Raymond Blanc reigns supreme. He was born in France 51 years ago and arrived in England at the age of 22 to learn the language and work in a small hotel on the river Thames. By 1984 he had become a first class chef and opened Le Manoir. It is a 16th century manor house, which has been modernised and is now very elegant, with 32 rooms and large gardens. Service is of a very high standard and of course the food is among the best. Raymond Blanc has created many new dishes and trained many leading chefs. A couple of his fish

dishes from the menu are seabass with langoustine and herb butter and millefeuille of red mullet. From the dessert menu: cassoulette nougatine or palette of sorbet.

Also recommended:

Fort William

Inverlochy Castle ★

Torlundy, 3 miles NE of Fort William, Scotland
Tel: 01397 702 177 Fax: 01397 702 953

A very luxurious castle hotel in the foothills of Ben Nevis, sitting amongst some of Scotland's finest scenery. Former owner Grete Hobbs raised cooking standards to star level.

Glasgow

Amaryllis ★

1Devonshire Gardens, Glasgow, Scotland
Tel: 0141 337 3434 Fax: 0141 339 0047

New name, new owner and new chef! The well-known One Devonshire Gardens has now become Amaryllis under the ownership of Gordon Ramsay. David Dempsey has arrived from Gordon's kitchen in London to be the new head chef. We expect great things from the new regime.

Great Malvern

Croque-en-Bouche ★1/2

221 Wells Road, Malvern Wells, Worcestershire
Tel: 01684 575859 Fax: 01684 560662

A remarkable and unusual restaurant with superb food, open for dinner only, Thursday to Saturday. Marion Jones cooks and her husband, Robin, takes care of wine and service. Excellent wine cellar with over 1,000 wines - 6 tables only so book way ahead.

Winteringham

Winteringham Fields ★★

Silver Street, Winteringham, North Lincolnshire
Tel: 01724 733 096 Fax: 01724 733 898

In the wilds of Lincolnshire Annie and Germain Schwab run one of the best restaurants in the country in a 16th century Grade II listed manor house. Full review in our next edition.

Greece (+30)

Athens

Boschetto
O

Alsos Evangelismou
Tel: 01 721 0893 Fax: 01 722 3598
(Closed Sunday)

At Boschetto you can eat under the trees of the grove of Evangelismou in summertime. It is a stylish restaurant specialising in Italian and Mediterranean cuisine, the best of its kind in Greece. Chef Dimitris Karayiannis will suggest some tempting dishes, among them cannelloni with sea gnocchi and gorgonzola sauce, or duck with figs and couscous. Another interesting dish is shrimps rolled in a lace cover of 'kadaifi'. The wine list includes some quite old Greek red wines - rather unusual.

Mezzo Mezzo
★

58 Syngrou Avenue
Tel: 01 924 444 Fax: 01 924 2716
(Dinner only, closed Sunday)

In a large and lofty restaurant with an open kitchen and many attractive paintings, chef Jean-Yves Caratoni prepares Italian and French dishes and also some eastern specialities. This is a very fashionable and popular establishment, open only for dinner. Among dishes that can be recommended is risotto with crayfish, rack of veal with caramelised onions or its Asian counterpart, imperial veal with dry sherry, and foie gras with pine kernels. Sommelier Nikos is in charge of an impressive underground wine cellar with a tasting lounge in front of it. Surprise: in summer the whole restaurant moves to a superb seaside location. Call and check before you go.

Spondi
★

5 Pyronos Street, Pangrati
Tel: 01 752 0658 Fax: 01 752 4021

Spondi is generally considered one of the best restaurants in Greece and it has recently been refurbished so that you now eat in an attractive room decorated with paintings by contemporary Greek artists. Chef Herve Ponzato presents some delicious dishes such as duck breast with honey, accompanied by spring rolls stuffed with spinach. John Dory fish is served with crispy fries, asparagus and a fine mustard, lemon and orange sauce - very original. There are good desserts such as soufflé au chocolat and a millefeuille with figs.

Vardis ★1/2

66 Diligianni Street, Kefalari
Tel: 01 623 0650 Fax: 01 801 0314
(Dinner only, closed Sunday)

Many of my Greek friends think that the starred Vardis may well serve the best food in Greece and I tend to agree - but note the food is French cooked by Jean de Grylleau. For Greek food look at other entries. Vardis is located in the Pendelikon hotel, at least half an hour from the city centre in the smart Kefalari district. In summer you eat in elegant marquees in the very attractive garden. Here are a few samples of the chef's creations: roulade de volaille au morilles, linguine with crayfish and foie gras salad with grapes marinated in dark sweet wine. There is an excellent list of French and Greek wines. The service is also very attentive. Reservations recommended.

White Elephant O

22 Timoleontos Vassou Street
Tel: 01 643 73024
(Closed Sunday)

This Elephant is situated in the charming Hotel Andromeda and is something as unusual as a Greek restaurant with Polynesian cuisine. It is considered to be among the top ten Athenean restaurants, also offering Thai and other Asian dishes. On the menu are spring rolls, classic crispy duck and marinated quails. Chef Toni Touan Dan also has other specialities for you to try. Contrary to the name the dining room is fairly small and intimate, as is the hotel with only just over 40 rooms.

Piraeus

Varoulko ★1/2

14 Deligiorgi
Tel: 01 411 2043 Fax: 01 422 1283
(Dinner only, closed Sunday)

Piraeus is the port of Athens, some ten kilometres south of the capital. The Florman recommendation is to go there and eat in Varoulko. Sit indoors or on the terrace and enjoy some very good cooking, mainly fish, by chef and owner Lefteris Lazarou. Dishes to try: cockles with sweet wine and garlic, marinated red mullet with beetroot cream or steamed angler fish with vegetables.

Vouliagmeni

The Club House ★

Astir Palace Hotel, Apollonos 40
Tel: 01 890 1784 Fax: 01 896 2582
(Only open May to October)
25 kms from Athens, along the coast, the Astir Palace is one of the finest hotels in Greece. Their Club House restaurant is on a verandah, literally hanging above the sea, with a breathtaking view over the Saronic Gulf. The Club House serves creative preparations of fresh fish and shellfish with live music. The Astir Palace resort is on a private promentary with 80 acres of private land. When I stayed here I found it a particularly relaxing weekend. I can recommend the fillet of red bream on a bed of rusti potatoes with ginger and saffron sauce, and try the 'surf and turf' which is beef filet and lobster tail with hot butter and bearnaise sauce. The carpaccio of seabass with olive oil and coriander is also very good.

Also recommended:

In Greece eating out at tavernas is very much a way of life. The Florman Guide has decided to list some of the best of the tavernas in the also recommended category. While the food and wine will be good do not expect tablecloths and linen napkins in these friendly places.

Athens

Frantzescos O

3 Skiathou Street, Kifissia
Tel: 01 620 4837
Simple décor and table settings, small wine list and good red carafe wine. Specialities from the island of Sifnos. Chickpeas, lamb cooked in red wine and dill, fresh fish, excellent grills and zvingi (a kind of doughnut) for dessert.

O Psaras O

54 Eleon Street, Kifissia
Tel: 01 620 5925
An excellent fish taverna in the northern suburb of Nea Kifissia. Fresh fish cooked to the customer's liking, fresh salads and a variety of seafood. The desserts are on the house. Small wine list.

O Serkos ke ta 4 Asteria

O

Zepou & 28, Xenofondos Street, Glyfada
Tel: 01 964 9553

An excellent taverna specializing in oriental cuisine. Baba ganouz, hummus, dolmadakia and excellent grilled meat. Oriental desserts to finish.

Spyros

O

17 Ethnikou Stratou Street, Ano Kifissia
Tel: 01 801 7869

This taverna also has simple décor and table settings, and quick service. Traditional Greek cuisine such as kokkoras pastitsada or fricassée avgolemono. Excellent salads, traditional desserts. Small, but well selected wine list.

Vlassis

O

8 Pasteur Street, Mavili Square
Tel: 01 646 3060

Classic Greek cooking, well presented in a simple taverna. Dishes such as minced meatballs in tomato sauce are very good. Note: in summertime Vlassis moves to the Zouberi area.

Skiathos

Limanakia

FF

Skiathos town Harbour
Tel: 0427 22835

Some of the best fresh cooking in Skiathos; reserve a table on the water's edge and choose from the fresh fish. My daughter-in-law's favourite; Nikos will look after you well.

Agnanti

FF

Evangelistria's Monastery road
Tel: 0427 22016

Wonderful balcony with a view over the town; good tyropita and excellent meat dishes. Essential to reserve; my son's favourite.

Greek menu terms

As Greek is a very difficult language for foreigners we are listing here some Greek menu terms translated into English, to help our readers:

Avgotaraho	Fish roe spread
Barbouni	Red Mullet
Briam	Vegetable stew
Dolmadakia	Stuffed vine leaves
Eliopsomo	Olive bread
Fagri	Couch's sea bream
Giouvetsi	Roast meat with pasta
Hortopita	Pie with wild greens
Hummus	Chickpea and tahini purée
Kakavia	Fish soup
Kalamarakia	Fried squid
Keftedes	Fried meatballs
Kontosouvli	Spit-roasted meat
Lahanodolmades	Stuffed cabbage leaves
Lathotyri	Cheese made with olive oil
Lavraki	Sea bass
Lithrini	Red bream
Marida	Whitebait
Melitzanokeftedes	Aubergine rissoles
Melitzanosalata	Aubergine purée
Mezedes	Titbits
Moussaka	Fried sliced aubergines and mince
Octapodi	Octopus
Panzeta	Pork belly
Peskandritsa	Monkfish
Revithokeftedes	Chickpea rissoles
Sardella	Sardine
Sargos	White bream
Skordalia	Garlic paste
Soutzoukakia	Meatballs in spicy tomato sauce
Souvlaki	Skewered meat
Spanakopita	Spinach pie in filo pastry
Spetzofai	Spicy sausage cooked with peppers
Stifado	Rabbit or beef and onion stew
Taramosalata	Fish roe purée
Tsipoura	Gilt head bream
Tyrokafteri	Spicy cheese purée
Tyropita	Cheese Pie in Filo Pastry
Tzatziki	Yoghurt with cucumber and garlic

Iceland (+354)

Food standards in Iceland are quite high and the Florman Guide has decided to be the first international restaurant guide to include a review of a few of the best restaurants in Reykjavik.

Reykjavik

The Gallery Restaurant ★

Hotel Holt, Bergstaoastraeti 37
Tel: 552 5700 Fax: 562 3025

The Hotel Holt is a small, intimate quality hotel with 42 rooms centrally located in a quiet street near the main business centre. The Gallery restaurant is known to be just about the best in the country for food, but it also has another claim to fame and that is a remarkable art gallery, the most important in Iceland. There are almost 400 works presenting a veritable panorama of modern Icelandic art from the 19th century to the present day. There are drawings and paintings also in the bar and in the hotel rooms. Turning to drinks the Gallery has a truly remarkable selection of cognacs and whiskies; there are 60 different cognacs to choose from and no less than 120 brands of malt whisky - that alone is worth a trip to Iceland! Two dishes to consider are: lightly smoked cod with leek and potato pureé with cep sauce and fried breast of duck with bacon polenta, pepper and potato purée and orange sauce.

Grillio ★

Radisson SAS Saga Hotel, Hagatorg
Tel: 525 9900 Fax: 525 9909
(Closed Monday)

On the top floor of this modern hotel with fine views over Reykjavik is the Grillio Restaurant - one of Iceland's best. The hotel is situated a few minutes from the city centre in the quiet grounds of the University of Iceland. For this coming winter the menu and the wine selection in the Grillio has been dedicated to Icelandic art and especially the painter Tolli. Chef de cuisine Bjarni Gunnar Kristinsson proposes some interesting dishes. Here is a selection: duck liver parfait and goose liver with grilled langoustines, fresh starry ray with herb 'beurre blanc' and potato purée or supreme of duck with exotic fruit and saffron sauce. Restaurant Manager Hendrik Hermannsson takes good care of the guests in the dining-room.

Humarhusio ★

Amtmannsstig 1

Tel: 561 3303 (no fax)

The name of this restaurant in English is the Lobster House. As Iceland is surrounded by some of the finest fishing waters anywhere it is not surprising that there is a quality restaurant with lobster in its name. Although there are a few meat dishes, lamb particularly, on the menu, the emphasis is very much on fish and shellfish. Here you can get the small sweet-tasting lobsters that are more delicate than those from warmer waters. Humarhusio likes to serve them poached and accompanied by a herb cream sauce. The restaurant is to be found in a restored 19th century house with character and charm. The next time I visit I would like to try cream of lobster soup followed by 'surf n'turf' which is grilled beef steak with grilled lobster tails, and then perhaps round this off with one of many chocolate desserts available.

Sommelier Brasserie O

Hverfisgata 46

Tel: 511 4455 Fax: 511 4456

(Closed Sunday)

As the name demonstrates this is a restaurant where wine is as important as the food. The two have always gone together - after all very few people enjoy a meal without wine. It may surprise readers living in continental Europe that there is a great deal of interest in Iceland in selecting, tasting and keeping quality wine. There is an association of Icelandic sommeliers and the president and founder is Harald Halldorsson, who is also co-owner of the Sommelier Brasserie. The other owner is Vignir Ormodsson who runs the restaurant. Head chef is young Robert Egilsson, who is a member of the Icelandic Culinary Youth Team and finally the Sommelier and Mâitre d' is Saevar Mar Sveinsson. Some examples from a five-course menu include: tiger prawns with gazpacho-shot and deep fried fennel in tempura, Cajun gumbo soup with tomatillo glaze, lamb T-bone with tamarind potatoes and garlic sauce and, to finish, chocolate 'Nirvana'.

Ireland (+353)

Dublin

The Commons O

85-86 St Stephen's Green
Tel: 01 478 0530 Fax: 01 478 0551
(Closed Saturday & Sunday)

This restaurant was formerly the college dining room of University College in a splendid Georgian period house. The basement restaurant has French doors opening onto a secluded south-facing terrace, where you can take your aperitif. There are tempting canapés and amuse bouche on arrival. Sebastian Masi, the chef, has a menu that is influenced by both French and Thai cuisine. Why not try seared king scallops with orange cardamom and vanilla dresssing or seared salmon rolled in sesame seeds with curried basmati and soya dressing. There is an excellent seven course tasting menu. Restaurant manager Michael Andrews supervises a pleasant restaurant with a nice atmosphere and good service.

Patrick Guilbaud ★★

21 Upper Merrion Street
Tel: 01 676 4192 Fax: 01 661 0052
(Closed Sunday & Monday)

In most countries there are a number of restaurateurs that compete for the top spot in cooking honours. In the Republic of Ireland Patrick Gilbaud and his chef Guillaume Lebrun are generally recognised as the best. I have certainly enjoyed my meals here tremendously. The cooking can best be described as French with Irish overtones. Naturally seafood features strongly on the menu. Last time I was there I had Dublin Bay prawns in filo pastry and roast scallops. A couple of years ago Gilbaud moved to his new location in the luxury Merrion Hotel, a restored Georgian town house opposite the government buildings. A good combination - the Merrion with its many facilities and Patrick Gilbaud with his superb restaurant.

Peacock Alley ★

St Stephen's Green
Tel: 01 478 7015 Fax: 01 478 7043
(Closed Saturday lunch & Sunday)

Conrad Gallagher is chef/patron of this large modern restaurant, excellently located on the first floor of the Fitzwilliam Hotel on the famous St Stephen's Green and with a separate entrance straight from the Green. One end

of the dining area looks over the Green while the other has a view of the white-tiled open kitchen. Gallagher started his cooking career in new York, becoming the chef of Hotel Waldorf Astoria's famous Peacock Alley Restaurant while still quite young. Opening in Dublin, he chose to retain the name. Conrad Gallagher is a somewhat controversial chef but his cooking is quite original and on balance he deserves his star.

Thornton's ★★

1 Portobello Road
Tel: 01454 9067 Fax: 01453 2947
(Closed Sunday & Monday)
Kevin Thornton is without doubt one of the finest chefs in Ireland today, and is well worth the two stars I am awarding him. His town-house restaurant is situated slightly out of the centre on the Union Canal. The bar and the kitchen are on the ground floor with two dining rooms upstairs. The cooking is modern Irish with French overtones and many fine dishes. Notable is his white asparagus mousse with a truffle vinaigrette. Another dish is roasted quail with onion tartlets and fresh girolle sauce. There is also a six-course tasting menu in smaller portions.

La Stampa O

35 Dawson Street
Tel: 01 677 8611 Fax: 01 677 3336
(Closed Saturday & Sunday lunch)
A dinner at La Stampa (in an elegant 19th century building just off Grafton Street) can be a romantic occasion. The restaurant has a very attractive interior with large mirrors, paintings and bronze sculptures by famous artists, and colourful gauze drapes swirling downwards from the magnificent ceiling. To celebrate their recent 10th anniversary chef Paul Catterson is presenting a new menu featuring tradtional European dishes with a dash of Eastern flavour : for example, roasted cod with red peppers and organic rack of lamb with sage jus. This is a fun and lively place that I recommend for an evening out.

Also recommended:

Les Frères Jacques O

74 Dame Street
Tel: 01 679 4555 Fax: 01 679 4725
A genuinely French restaurant with French staff. The menu is well balanced, specialising in fish. Note the lobster tank outside.

Italy (+39)

Rome

La Pergola ★★

The Cavalieri Hilton, Via Cadiolo 101
Tel: 06 350 91 Fax: 06 3509 2165

Although Hilton Hotels always keep high standards it is very rare to find one with a superb gourmet restaurant. Well, Rome is one exception and La Pergola is the restaurant. The Hilton is built on Monte Mario, one of the seven hills surrounding Rome. Situated on the roof garden La Pergola has an unparalleled view of the Eternal City. Surprisingly the chef is a young German from Bavaria, Heinz Beck, 35. He is being talked of as the leading chef in Rome and I think he deserves two stars, but you have to decide for yourself. Do try the seven-course gourmet menu, which includes filet of sole with fines herbes and venison in a salt crust with pistachios.

Relais le Jardin ★

Hotel Lord Byron, Via De Notaris 5
Tel: 06 322 0404 Fax: 06 322 0405
(Closed Sunday)

Lord Byron is a small (37 rooms), quiet, and a very exclusive hotel with an excellent garden restaurant. It can be found in the Pasioli hills, close to the Villa Borghese. It is definitely an 'in' place. The restaurant has an imaginative cuisine with a Roman flair. Try risotto or fleurs de courgette, artichokes with black truffles and carré d'agneau croustillant. The armagnac soufflé is a good way to end the meal.

Roof Garden Restaurant FF

Hotel Hassler Villa Medici, Piazza Trinità dei Monti 6
Tel: 06 69 93 40 Fax: 06 67 89 991

On my visits to Rome I have occasionally been able to stay at the charming and luxurious Hassler which has a marvellous position at the top of the famous Spanish Steps and next to the Trinita dei Monte Church. It was the favourite hotel of the late Swedish King, Gustaf V1 Adolf, who stayed here regularly. The roof restaurant is one of my favourites with its fabulous view of the city. The food is, as you would expect, classic Italian of a good standard. The service is, as you might also expect, very attentive.

Canneto sull'Oglio

Dai Pescatore ★★★

Via Runate 17
Tel: 0376 723 001 Fax: 0376 703 04
(Closed Monday, Tuesday, 3 weeks in January & August)
In the picturesque village of Canneto, in the Oglio Park Reserve by the river Oglio, this restaurant has been owned and run by the Santin family since 1920. Signora Nadia Santin cooks to a three star standard in this remarkable restaurant. She is one of a small group of female three star chefs in Italy. The cooking here is Italian cuisine at the highest level - a place not to be missed. Nadia's husband, Antonio Santin, is the owner and also runs the restaurant. He has a wonderful wine cellar with many rare vintages.

Cernobbio

Villa d'Este ★

Via Regina 40
Tel: 031 3481 Fax: 031 348 844
(Only open March-November)
It takes only a short hour by car north of Milan to reach the splendid atmospheric Hotel Villa d'Este, beautifully positioned on Lake Como with indoor and outdoor swimmming pools and gardens down to the lake. There are two restaurants, the Verandah that looks over the lake and is my favourite, and also the Grill Room. The service is first class. I have stayed here many times enjoying good modern Italian food and mainly Italian wines.

Chiavari

Ca Peo ★

Via dei Caduti 80
Tel: 0185 31 96 96 Fax: 0185 31 96 71
(Closed Monday & Tuesday lunch & November)
If I have one favourite restaurant in the province of Liguria it is Ca Peo, owned and run by Franco Solari. It is a simple restaurant in a small hill town high above the resorts of Rapallo and Portofino. My wife and I have eaten and stayed overnight here many times. I first heard about Franco Solari from my friend the famous American journalist Johnny Apple who went there and wrote about it in the 1980's. It is refreshing to find a good restaurant away from the tourist areas of the Mediterranean coast. Ca Peo has a breathtaking view of the hills and the sea and excellent food. I advise you to put yourself in the hands of Mr

Solari and let him compose a menu for you of many small specialities of the day. The cooking is done by Signora Solari.

Erbusco

Gualtiero Marchesi ★★1/2

Via Vittorio Emanuele 11
Tel: 030 776 0562 Fax: 030 776 03 79
(Closed Sunday dinner, Monday & 3 weeks in January)

Some years ago when 'cuisine nouvelle' was in fashion in France Gualtiero Marchesi was in the forefront in introducing 'la cuisina nova' to Italians in his well-known restaurant in Milan. I used to enjoy eating there but Italian opinion swung against this French import. All that is history and Marchesi is now cooking in the restaurant named after him in the Hotel L'Albereta and showing the brilliance of his talent. To enjoy Marchesi's inventive food you should stay in the hotel with its elegant bedrooms and many facilities such as an indoor swimming pool, a spa, riding, sailing, and golf. There are lovely views from the hilltop location. Gualtiero Marchesi cooks at the upper end of the two star rating, thus I award him two and a half stars.

Florence

Enoteca Pinchiorri ★★★

Via Ghibellina 87
Tel: 055 242 777 Fax: 055 244 983
(Closed Sunday, Monday, Wednesday lunch & August)

This is one of my absolute favourites in Italy. Beautifully situated in a 15th century Florentine palace in the bustling city centre, but there is a calm interior courtyard where meals are served in summertime. There are also several attractive and well decorated dining rooms. Enoteca does of course mean wine cellar and the cellars that Giorgio Pinchiorri has at his disposal contain around 150,000 bottles which makes it not only one of the best but probably the largest restaurant cellar in Italy. Giorgio's French-born wife Annie Feolde is in charge of the kitchen and the combination makes this one of Italy's best restaurants. The last time my wife and I visited we dined in the courtyard on some marvellous dishes such as sea bass baked in a salt crust with tomato, olive sauce and mullet roe with deep fried mozarella-stuffed aubergine. There is also a menu with traditional Tuscan dishes. Make sure you don't miss this place.

Villa San Michele ★

Via Doccia 4, Fiesole
Tel: 055 567 8200 Fax: 055 567 8250
(Closed January & February)

On one of my visits to Florence I decided to escape the heat by staying outside the town on one of the surrounding hills. The logical choice was the historic Villa San Michele which is a beautiful 16th century Tuscan villa with a façade designed by Michelangelo. It has stunning views over Florence, luxurious rooms, a heated swimming pool, a gym and a piano bar. There is an indoor restaurant and an outdoor loggia. You can choose from a selection of Tuscan culinary delights such as tagliatelle with lobster, ravioli with aubergine and various risottos. There is a comprehensive list of regional wines.

Milan

Aimo e Nadia ★★

Via Montecuccoli 6
Tel: 02 41 68 86 Fax: 02 48 30 20 05
(Closed Saturday lunch, Sunday & August)

Milan's best cuisine is a long way from the centre in a somewhat dull residential neighbourhood - but it is worth the journey so that you can enjoy the cooking of Aimo and his wife Nadia Moloni. There are only 36 seats in two small dining rooms decorated with modern paintings, so book ahead. When I was there recently I ordered green lasagna with watercress and sea anenomes with ricotta and fresh tomatoes.

Antica Osteria del Ponte ★★★

Piazza G. Negri, Cassinetta di Lugagnano
Tel: 02 942 0034 Fax: 02 942 0610
(Closed Sunday, Monday & August)

To have the finest possible meal in the Milan area you have to take a short trip, 20 kms (12 miles) south west of Milan to Cassinetta di Lugagnano. There you will find a traditional country inn with pink brick walls, three dining rooms and a lovely terrace with a small waterfall. You can eat on the terrace in good weather. The Santin family will look after you with Ezio Santin in the kitchen with his son Maurizio. Signora Renata Santin takes care of the guests in the dining room. The cooking is rich and imaginative, for example tarte de pâtes fraîches à la gourge et truffes blanches.

Beoucc
O

Piazza Belgioioso 2
Tel: 02 760 20 224 Fax: 02 796 173
(Closed Saturday & Sunday lunch)

Quite simply the oldest restaurant in Milan (300 years) located on an attractive square near La Scala Opera House. Beoucc serves classic Italian cuisine including some typical Milanese dishes. The service is friendly and attentive and in the summer meals can be eaten in the garden. In addition to all the classic pasta dishes you have a choice of bream filet with shrimps or sea bass with courgettes. A good meat dish is lamb cutlets with hollandaise sauce. This restaurant is a favourite of Milanese business people.

Biffi Scala-Tuolà
FF

Piazza della Scala
Tel: 02 86 66 51 Fax: 02 86 66 53
(Closed Sunday)

If you are heading for the famous La Scala Opera House you can treat yourself to an excellent dinner, before or after the performance, at Biffi Scala-Tuolà. This restaurant was opened soon after the Opera house, and is in the same building. Their specialities are classic Milanese and Lombardy dishes, and the desserts are particularly good, for example pear and pistachio torte or their famous torte Biffi Scala which is puff pastry with raspberries and cream.

Giannino
★

Via Amatore Sciesa 8
Tel: 02 55 19 55 82 Fax: 02 55 19 57 90
(Closed Sunday & Monday)

Here is a classic Milanese restaurant which has recently celebrated its centenary. This beautiful restaurant with several dining rooms is a must for any visitor to Milan. You can see through to the kitchen watching the chefs at work. There is a also a winter garden. New chef Davide Oldani has some interesting specialities, for example steamed lobster in a pastry crust. The wine list features naturally mostly Italian wines. Free private parking.

Savini
★

Galleria Vittorio Emanuele II
Tel: 02 72 00 34 33 Fax: 02 72 02 28 88
(Closed Sunday & August)

Restaurant Savini is an institution in Milan with elaborate décor, characteristic of its 19th century roots, with turn of the century glittering chandeliers and plush red carpets. It is attractively located in the Galleria Vittorio Emanuele II,

where all visitors like to walk. The cooking is very traditional. Milanese specialities like rice fried like a pancake or ossobucco (veal braised with orange zest, tomato, onions and garlic) are excellent choices. The service is excellent. Booking is advisable.

Sant'Agata sui Due Golfi

Don Alfonso 1890 ★★★

Corso Sant'Agata 11

Tel: 081 878 0026 Fax: 081 533 0226

(Closed January/February)

There are very few gastronomic temples in the southernmost part of Europe. The exception to this is the marvelllous Don Alfonso in the little town of Sant'Agata on top of the hill between Sorrento and Positano. Take the Naples/Salerno motorway, exit at Castellamare, then go up the hill from Meta de Sorrento. Founded, as the name shows, in 1890 by grandfather Alfonso it is now in the hands of Alfonso Iaccarino in the kitchen while his charming and attractive wife Livia looks after the dining room. There are five large hotel rooms above the restaurant so my wife and I were able to first dine and then stay on for a lighter lunch the next day. We also visited the large underground wine cellar. The food is very much Mediterranean which is complemented with home produced olive oil and fresh vegetables from their own farm.

Soriso

Al Sorriso ★★★

Via Roma 18

Tel: 03 22 98 32 28 Fax: 03 22 98 33 28

(Closed Monday & Tuesday lunch)

The Italian lakes in the foothills of the Alps form a lovely tourist area. There are of course hundreds of inns and restaurants around the lakes but let us take a look at hotel/restaurant Al Sorriso, in the little town of Soriso (yes, one R only) above the Lago di Orta, the smallest of the lakes. Here a remarkable lady chef and her husband, Lusia and Angelo Valazza, run a small hotel with one of the finest restaurants in Italy. We drove up from Milan (taking under two hours) and spent a enjoyable weekend relaxing and eating. The service is very personal and efficient. The cooking could be described as 'Haute Italian' with some very delicate dishes and taste sensations. As there are only eight bedrooms, and you will certainly want to stay overnight as my wife and I did, book well ahead.

Turin

Balbo ★

Via Andrea Doria 11
Tel: 011 839 5775 Fax: 011 815 1042
(Closed Monday & 3 weeks in July/August)
The Piedmont region in north-west Italy is known for good regional food including the famous white truffle from Alba. Turin, without reaching gastronomic heights, has some excellent restaurants serving good quality food. Balbo is a good exponent of 'cuccina del territorio' and may serve the best food in Turin. It is set elegantly in an 18th century palace in the centre of town. Some of the dishes on offer are fresh tagliatelle with egg yolk, vegetables, pine nuts and raisins or crayfish with a wild rice salad. There are fixed price menus available. Reservations recommended.

Venice

Harry's Bar ★

Calle Vallaresso 1323, San Marco
Tel: 041 528 57 77 Fax: 041 520 88 22
There are not many restaurants as famous as Harry's Bar. It is known and loved by people from many countries. I know people who make special trips there every year. A Swedish friend of mine will fly in and take the vaporetto (water bus) straight to Harry's then have a long pleasant lunch and fly back! It is owned by Arrigo (Harry in Italian) Cipriani and was started by his late father known as the "Commendatore". There is a world famous dish and a cocktail both created by Cipriani senior. The cocktail is the Bellini - peach juice and Prosecco, Italian sparkling wine. The dish is Carpaccio - thin slices of raw beef filet, marinated. Both were named after famous Venetian painters. The restaurant has a nice downstairs bar, serving the driest Martinis and then you can eat upstairs or downstairs (downstairs is more 'in') looking out over the Grand Canal.

Also recommended:

Corte Sconta FF

Calle del Pestrin 3886
Tel: 041 522 20 24
Some of the best food in Venice; modern and very popular. Book well in advance.

Harry's Dolci ★

Giudecca 773

Tel: 041 522 48 44 Fax: 041 522 23 22

Take the vaporetto over to Giudecca. Impeccable service, good food. Owned by the Cipriani family.

Ventimiglia

Baia Beniamin FF

Tel: 0184 381 32 Fax: 0184 380 02

(Closed Sunday dinner & Monday)

Of all the restaurants reviewed in this guide this is the only one on a beach. Yes, surprisingly a first class restaurant right on the beach, but it is a private beach. It is quite difficult to find and you may have to enquire when booking, but you turn off from highway Europa 63 (the coast road), half a mile from the French border, and slowly descend a narrow road towards the sea and the car park. Then continue walking down steps to the beach restaurant, surrounded by eucalyptus trees and tropical flowers. We usually have a swim before enjoying a lunch with excellent seafood and good Ligurian wine.

Balzi Rossi ★1/2

Via Balzi Rossi 2-Ponte San Ludivico

Tel: 0184 381 32 Fax: 0184 385 32

(Closed Monday & Tuesday lunch)

This is an Italian restaurant a few yards from France! If you come by car from Menton, the border town, and cross into Italy, Balzi Rossi is immediately after the border post on the right. An unusual location but a good place for your first meal in Italy. The restaurant is right by the sea with a terrace and a fine view over the Meditteranean. The family Beglia will cook for you and look after you in the dining room. Recommended dishes: shellfish soup, courgette flowers with a shellfish mousse and large prawns lightly pan fried, or octopus salad with white beans. Like most restaurants on the sea they also have sea bass (loup de mer).

Also recommended:

Porto Ercole

Il Pellicano FF

Strada Panorimaca
Tel: 0564 85 81 11 Fax: 0564 83 34 18
A charming seaside resort hotel on a scenic hillside overlooking the Meditteranean some 100 miles from Rome. Excellent restaurant offering barbecue buffets and candle-lit dinners.

Portofino

Hotel Splendido ★1/2

Viale Baratta 16
Tel: 0185 26 78 01 Fax: 0185 26 90 24
The most luxurious hotel on the Italian Riviera near Genoa. First class restaurant with breathtaking views over the sea.

The Netherlands (+31)

The Hague

Hotel des Indes ★

Lange Voorhout 54
Tel: 070 361 2345 Fax: 070 345 721
(Closed Saturday lunch & Sunday)
This is a gracious hotel, built in the 19th century, and located on the most prestigious square in the Hague. It also has a good restaurant. This is where I stay, and eat, when visiting this lovely city. The whole hotel was renovated a few years ago after being taken over by the InterContinental hotel group. The restaurant, as so often in the Netherlands, serves predominately French cuisine, with a Mediterranean touch. The chef, however, is a Dutchman, Martin Ozinga. On Martin's current menu are dishes such as warm goat's cheese with ruccola, courgette and a vinaigrette of lentils, a bisque of langoustines with fennel and coriander, pike-perch with caraway, shallots and Pinot Noir sauce or Barbary duck served with duck liver, sauce hollandaise and a red wine syrup.

Also recommended:

Da Roberto O

Noordeinde 196
Tel: 070 346 4977 Fax: 070 362 5286
Roberto De Luca serves good traditional Italian food in this attractively re-decorated air-conditioned restaurant.

Amsterdam

Café Roux ★1/2

Grand Hotel, O.Z. Voorburgwal 197
Tel: 020 555 3560 Fax: 020 555 3222
Albert Roux and I have been friends for many years and I congratulate the inhabitants of Amsterdam in having Roux as a consultant chef at this excellent and lively restaurant. The resident chef is Andrew Gaskell. The Café Roux is part of the Grand Hotel which was created ten years ago by converting the old town hall into a luxury hotel. Part of this attractive building is from the 16th century but most of it is modern. It features a mural by a famous artist, Karel Appel, stained glass windows and Gobelin tapestries. The reception areas and bedrooms were designed by Monique Roux, wife of Albert. There is also an interior garden next to the canal. Café Roux has an informal brasserie atmosphere with oak floors and an art deco interior design. It

overlooks a picturesque canal. The cuisine is French and features some of Albert's special dishes such as soufflé Suisesse, one of my absolute favourites (a floating cheese soufflé in a creamy Gruyère sauce). Another starter is a crispy pastry galette with grilled vegetables, marinated goats cheese and a black olive dressing. A main course to mention is poached fillets of sole with sauce Nantua.

Christophe ★

Leliegracht 46
Tel: 020 625 0807 Fax: 020 638 9132
(Dinner only, closed Sunday & Monday)

Jean-Christophe Royer, chef/patron, cooked in Paris and New York before opening his own restaurant in Amsterdam in 1987. It quickly became a success and now ranks as one of the best eating places in town. The split-level dining room is unusual and looks out over a small canal. No doubt influenced by his French-Algerian background, Jean-Christophe specializes in French food with a Mediterranean accent. One interesting starting dish is a tartare of salmon, smoked salmon and salmon caviar. Then you could try loin of lamb in a pepper crust or the foie gras marinated in sweet and spicy wine.

Excelsior ★

Hotel Europe, Nieuwe Doelenstraat
Tel: 020 531 1705 Fax: 020 531 1778
(Closed Saturday lunch)

This hotel is right on the intersection of two canals and there is a fine view over the water and the passing boats from both the restaurant and most rooms. This is where I normally stay when visiting Amsterdam, partly because of its location right in the centre, and partly because of the high standard of Restaurant Excelsior. The dining room has chandeliers, tall candelabras and piano music, and the tables are well spaced. The cooking is French with several fixed price menus. The wine cellar is one of the best with no less than 30,000 bottles. There is also an informal brasserie, Le Relais, with lower prices and no dress code.

La Rive ★★

Hotel Amstel, Prof. Tulpplein 1
Tel: 020 622 6060 Fax: 020 622 5808
(Closed Saturday lunch & Sunday)

The Amstel ranks as one of the most luxurious hotels in the Netherlands and its many facilities and quiet location right on the river Amstel makes it very desirable. The biggest attraction, however, may be the superb restaurant, La

Rive, attractively situated on the river level with a fine view. Recently appointed chef Edwin Kats has kept the standard high and the food may be just about the best in Amsterdam. The menu offers many interesting dishes and I have selected the following for my readers to consider: sea bream prepared in a salt crust with a compote of artichoke, tomato, sweet pepper, shallots and balsamic vinegar, 'Waterlant's loin of veal prepared with cloves and bay-leaf, celery and marrow or roast Barbary duck caramelised with spices. For dessert I suggest cinnamon puff pastry with poached apples and prunes, cinnamon juice and caramel ice-cream. Remember to enquire about the 'chef's table': this seats six and is next to the open kitchen so you can watch the chefs at work.

Also recommended:

Vermeer O

Prins Henrikkade 59

Tel: 020 556 4885 Fax: 020 556 4858

Within the hotel Barbizon Palace, Restaurant Vermeer (named of course after the famous artist) occupies three restored 17th century canal houses with antiques and wooden panelling. Classical cooking with some Italian influence.

Bosch en-Duin

de Hoefslag ★

Vosenlaan 28

Tel: 030 225 10 51 Fax: 030 228 58 21

(Closed Sunday)

When driving through Holland some time ago I came across this charming small hotel with a fine restaurant. I have since been back to enjoy again the very good food offered. de Hoefslag is in the middle of the woods, a few kilometres east of Utrecht and some 55 kms south-east of Amsterdam. In good weather you can lunch or dine on the terrace, shaded by trees. There is also a bistro for simpler meals. Unusually this restaurant also offers a vegetarian menu which looks quite tempting. It features salad with brie and truffles, watercress soup and asparagus with holllandaise. I wish more restaurants would oblige the growing number of vegetarians with special menus. If you are driving through Holland this is a lovely place to visit.

Haarlem

De Bokkedoorns ★★

Zeeweg 53
Tel: 023 526 3600 Fax: 023 527 3143
(Closed Saturday lunch & Monday)

Relaxing on the terrace of this gourmet restaurant you have a unique view of sand dunes and the lake beyond. The dunes are so close that you can almost reach out and touch them. It is a perfect setting for a fine meal not far from the bustle of Amsterdam and Haarlem. Proprietor John Beeren runs one of the best restaurants in the country with a very creative kitchen. Chef Lucas Rive presents dishes such as lukewarm marinated Irish salmon with deep fried wild oysters and cauliflower cream, dry fried fillet of monkfish garnished with Patanegra ham and snails in a light garlic sauce. For dessert try raspberries with a vanilla and fresh lavender cream, filo pastry crisps and raspberry sorbet.

Kruiningen

Manoir Inter Scaldes ★

Zandweg 2
Tel: 0113 38 1753 Fax: 0113 38 1763
(Closed Monday & Tuesday)

A beautiful manor house in the southern Netherlands near one of the most attractive river deltas in Europe. The house has a picturesque thatched roof and is set in lovely gardens. The owners are Kees and Maartje Boudeling and Mrs Boudeling is the highly skilled chef. Being on Zeeland and so near the river Schelde it is quite natural that various fish dishes are the main feature of the cooking. A good starting dish is hot Zeeland oysters in vinaigrette or marinated scallops. Other mouth-watering offerings are smoked lobster with caviar sauce and turbot with truffles. The meal tastes even better taken in the garden restaurant. There are 12 hotel rooms if you wish to prolong your stay. I suggest asking for directions when booking.

Rotterdam

Parkheuvel ★★

Heuvellaan 21
Tel: 010 436 0766 Fax: 010 436 7140
(Closed Saturday lunch & Sunday)

There is no finer restaurant in this city than Parkheuvel, owned by Cees and Rosalie Helder. It is also well situated in a modern semi-circular building with large windows, overlooking the river Maas and the harbour. In summertime you can sit on a lovely terrace outside. Incidentally, the harbour of Rotterdam is the world's largest. Chef Cees Helder changes the menu daily in order to utilise the very freshest produce from the market, such as scallops, sole and turbot. Helder also uses truffles quite a lot in his cooking. There are several set menus to choose from but an interesting dish is sweetbread with truffles and sauce Perigordine. Cherries grilled with marzipan and champagne is a most unusual dessert.

Valkenburg

Juliana ★1/2

Prinses Juliana Hotel, Broekhem 11
Tel: 043 601 2244 Fax: 043 601 4405
(Closed Saturday lunch)

In the south-east corner of the Netherlands, near Maastricht, there is an excellent Relais & Chateaux hotel with a very fine restaurant. The Prinses Juliana was founded by the Stevens family back in 1914. It is still family-owned and is now in the capable hands of Paul and Doris Stevens. The hotel recently underwent a full restoration. The restaurant and its terrace look out over a beautiful garden. In the summer meals are served outside and if the weather changes a glass roof will protect the guests. My family and I have stopped over here and enjoyed the comfortable accommodation but more specifically came to enjoy the food. The restaurant has the reputation of being one of the best in the country. Some of the dishes on offer: sautéed langoustine tails with poached eggs and goose liver, followed by grilled turbot à la mousseline or you could have a meat dish such as duck confit with cream of truffles.

Norway (+47)

Oslo

Annen Etage ★

Hotel Continental, Stortingsgaten 24-26
Tel: 22 82 40 00 Fax: 22 42 96 89
(Dinner only, closed Sunday)

Annen Etage means second floor and that is where you will find this classic hotel restaurant. The cuisine is French but with many Norwegian specialities. Chef Morten Hallan proposes fricassée of mussels and fennel with pickled ginger and mussel sauce, pan-fried dorade with sweetbread and glazed parsley or carré of red deer. General manager Nicolas Facchin Blomgren is in charge of one of the most attractive and stylish hotel dining rooms in the whole of Scandinavia.

Bagatelle ★★1/2

Bygdøy Allé 3
Tel: 22 12 14 40 Fax: 22 43 64 20
(Dinner only, closed Sunday & 4 weeks July/August)

Chef/patron Eyvind Hellstrøm has a formidable reputation in Norway. He creates classic French cuisine using the finest raw materials, especially fish and shellfish, but he also serves reindeer meat. Hellstrøm trained with the great Fredy Girardet in Switzerland before starting in Oslo in the early eighties. Bagatelle is stylish, with rose coloured carpets and pale yellow walls hung with striking modern paintings from local galleries, which change every month. The china is in unusually strong colours and service is also of a high standard. Now that you are seated comfortably what do you consider eating? May I suggest ordering either the five or the seven course tasting menu which will include shellfish dishes such as perhaps grilled crayfish or carpaccio of scallops. A good fish to choose is cod roasted in its skin with truffle butter. I have enjoyed several superb meals here.

Le Canard ★

President Harbitz Gate 4
Tel: 22 54 34 00 Fax: 22 54 34 10
(Dinner only, closed Sunday)

An attractive, spacious villa from 1899 is the home of Le Canard. It is surrounded by a nice garden and a private car park. The interior is rather unusual but quite appealing with a mixture of furniture in different styles. The cooking by chef Trond Andresen is more traditional with several dishes based on duck. Try, for example canard rôti aux olives. A recommended fish course is roast turbot with truffles. Those readers who like soufflés, as I do, must try the after eight chocolate and mint soufflé. The wine cellar has over twenty thousand bottles so there is a wide choice. Dinner only

Oro ★

Tordenskiolds Gate 6A
Tel: 23 01 02 40 Fax: 23 01 02 48
(Closed July)

Norwegian chefs have scored extremely well in the famous international cookery competition 'Bocuse d'Or'. Terje Ness, the chef at Oro, won a gold medal in the 1999 competition which is a great achievement considering that Norway's gastronomic scene is fairly small. So hurry to Oro to taste the food. Here the kitchen is open so that the guests can look directly at the chefs preparing their dinner. The starters are particularly good, among them oysters and scallops. A main course I recommend is carré of lamb with coriander and lime. An unusual dessert is chocolate sorbet with eucalyptus.

Spisestedet Feinschmecker ★

Balchensgate 5
Tel: 22 44 17 77 Fax: 22 56 11 39
(Closed Sunday)

Spisestedet is Norwegian for 'eating-place' and Feinschmecker is German for gourmet; the two certainly come together here - this is a restaurant for gourmets who enjoy the masterly cooking of Lars Erik Underthun - an internationally renowned chef. Lars Erik has represented Norway in the 'cooking olympics'. So come on in and sit down in this tastefully decorated grey and red dining room, with antique Norwegian furniture and shelves filled with silver and old glass. As always, Norway being so close to the sea, fish and shellfish is a very good choice but there are also many excellent meat dishes.

Statholdergaarden ★

Rådhusgate 11
Tel: 22 41 88 00 Fax: 22 41 22 24
(Closed Sunday)

Chef/proprietor Bent Stiansen has a great reputation in Norway as one of the country's best chefs. He was the first Scandinavian chef to win the gold medal in the famous Bocuse d'Or cookery competition in 1993. The restaurant is in one of the oldest houses in Oslo, beautifully decorated in 18th century style with many fine ornate stucco ceilings. Meals are served in 5 small dining rooms. The menu changes often, depending on the season. Stiansen uses mainly Norwegian produce for his French/European cooking. I would like to recommend dishes such as shellfish consommé with grilled scallops and wild mushrooms, spicy duck liver on a bed of caramelised onions. An excellent fish course is grilled turbot served with dill sauce, spinach and garlic cauliflower.

Also recommended:

Theatercaféen FF

Stortingsgaten 24-26
Tel: 22 82 40 50 Fax: 22 41 20 94

This is a large, Viennese style café on the ground floor of the Hotel Continental. A favourite meeting place for the Oslo 'in' crowd. At lunchtime there are good open sandwiches.

Portugal (+351)

Lisbon

Casa da Comida ★★

Travessa das Amoreiras 1
Tel: 21 388 5376 Fax: 21 387 5132
(Closed Saturday lunch & Sunday)

Many consider this the best restaurant in Lisbon and I tend to agree. It is a peaceful and attractive place where you sit comfortably on Regency furniture, looking out over the flower filled courtyard with a tiled fountain. When I visit Lisbon I tend to make this my first port of call. At the start of the meal you may enjoy an amuse bouche such as seafood fritters or salmon ravioli. Fish is a speciality and I can recommend, as a starter, hot prawns in garlic and then for a main course perhaps grilled sole or turbot in a green pepper sauce. There is an excellent wine list with many Portuguese specialities. The port wine is good and reasonably priced. Reservations recommended.

Gambrinus ★

Rua das portas de Santo Antao 25
Tel: 21 342 1466 Fax: 21 346 5032

If it is fish and shellfish you are thinking of Gambrinus is your place. Traditional Portuguese food is served such as crème de mariscos which is shellfish soup or you can try seabass in a clam sauce. The desserts are interesting but classical, such as chocolate soufflé or crepe suzette. This is a bustling place, always busy, right in the centre of town. If you are in a hurry you can eat and drink at the bar counter.

O Faz Figura FF

Rua do Paraíso 15-B
Tel: 21 886 8981 Fax: 21 886 8981
(Closed Sunday)

Sitting on the terrace of this lovely restaurant one has a fine view of the River Tagus and the harbour area below. Inside there are two air-conditioned dining rooms with leather Chesterfield banquettes which gives this restaurant a club-like atmosphere. The food is typically Portuguese with dishes such as tiny grilled squid, salad of gambas and portuguese steak cooked in a casserole with smoked ham. The wines are mainly Portuguese. The service is friendly and attentive. I have enjoyed several pleasant meals here.

Pap'acorda FF

Rua da Atalaia 57-59

Tel: 21 346 4811 Fax: 21 342 97 05

To reach Pap'acorda you have to penetrate narrow streets of the fashionable Bairo Alto quarter, one of the seven hills of Lisbon. Under the direction of Jose Miranda and Fernando Fernandes it is a well run restaurant which I enjoy as it is so different. One of the reasons for coming here is to eat acorda - an extraordinary mixture of bread, egg, oil, garlic and coriander, stuffed into lobster or prawns. You can also enjoy good shellfish. A typical dess-sert is chocolate mousse. The wines are of course Portuguese. Friendly service. Do book ahead.

Tágide ★

Largo da Académia, Nacional de Belas Artes 18

Tel: 21 342 0720 Fax: 21 347 1880

(Closed Saturday & Sunday)

High up on a hill with a fabulous view over the river Tajus and the harbour, this is a good place to both eat and relax. I have several times chosen Tagide to entertain Portuguese friends. In the elegant dining room there are classic paintings, a fountain from 1677 and a collection of eighteenth century tile murals. The menu specialises in traditional Portuguese regional fare such as smoked swordfish. As is typical in Portugal there are also many variations of cod on the menu. You will also find some international dishes. Several great wines can be found on the wine list. Booking recommended.

Tavares ★

Rua da Misericórdia 37

Tel: 21 342 1112 Fax: 21 347 8125

(Closed Saturday & Sunday lunch)

History and opulence characterise Lisbon's oldest restaurant, founded in 1784. It is located in the old town in a splendid 16th century building. The décor is classical with long empire-style mirrors and chandeliers - and the food is good too. Tavares may be rather formal but I enjoy eating here - now and then it is nice to go to a more formal place. The menu mixes French and Portuguese dishes such as foie gras, brochette of gambas, supreme of sea bream florentine, quail with cherries and duck with orange.

Also recommended:

Clara
O

Campo dos Mártires da Pátria 49

Tel: 21 885 3053 Fax: 21 885 2082

A former private house with a floodlit garden converted into an elegant restaurant, with excellent Portuguese specialities such as smoked swordfish.

Conventual
O

Praça das Flores 45

Tel: 21 390 9196 Fax: 21 390 9196

A former bakery in the old quarter featuring traditional Portuguese dishes. Good value menus.

Pabe
O

Rua Duque de Palmela 27

Tel: 21 353 7484 Fax: 21 353 6439

As the name implies this is a popular English pub but it is also a good restaurant with shellfish specialities.

Porto de Santa Maria
★

Cascais, near Lisbon

Tel: 21 487 0240 Fax: 21 458 0949

Possibly the best seafood served in a large restaurant on a beach facing the sea.

Spain (+34)

Madrid

Casa Lucio ★

Cava Baja 35
Tel: 91 365 3252 Fax: 91 366 4866
(Closed Saturday lunch)

Casa Lucio is an excellent place to go to if you wish to eat typical Castillian cuisine, prepared by chef Aurelio Calderón. It is located near the Plaza Mayor, the busy central area of Madrid. Patron Lucio has managed to make this a very 'in' restaurant and it is said that King Juan Carlos likes to eat here. The most favoured tables are on the ground floor near the front bar but not the upstairs area. Castillian dishes are rather robust such as tripe Madrid style with a rich tomato sauce with garlic.

El Amparo ★★

Puigcerdá 8
Tel: 91 431 6456 Fax: 91 575 5491
(Closed Saturday lunch & Sunday)

The setting is very attractive; dining on three floors with a glass roof overlooking an open atrium. Try to sit as high up as possible. The cooking is from the Basque region under the guidance of famous chef Martin Berasategui. The in-house chef is young Ignacio Perez Lecea. The restaurant is managed by Senora Carmen Guasp who welcomes and looks after the guests. I have enjoyed several meals here and would like to recommend dishes such as sea bass with clams, lobster with tuna mousse and oven-baked stuffed crab. Sommelier Luis Miguel will give you good advice on what wines to choose. This is definitely one of the best restaurants in Madrid, worth its two stars.

El Bodegón ★

Pinar 15
Tel: 91 562 3137 Fax: 91 562 9725
(Closed Saturday lunch, Sunday & August)

If you are looking for classic Basque cuisine with traditional décor this is the place for you. Chefs Hilario Arbelaitz and José Machado prepare high quality regional dishes - try sea-bass with carrot juice and shallot oil. A selection from the excellent dessert menu is caramelised pineapple with a scoop of warm chocolate. The wine cellar is superb with a vast selection of Spanish wines. El Bodegón has the feel of a gentleman's club - lots of oak panelling and cigar smoke!

La Broche ★★

Miguel Angel 29-31
Tel & Fax: 91 399 3778
(Closed Saturday lunch, Sunday & August)

Sergi Ariola, 31, is the young, much talked about star chef of this restaurant. His former teacher and his idol is Ferran Adria of El Bulli who is the most famous chef in Spain today (see separate entry). Sergi is being mentioned as the next Adria. We will follow him in years to come. Today La Broche will delight you, with some inspired dishes such as sea bass with onions soaked in curry sauce, duck liver pie with olive oil or a simple dish, sardines marinated with herring eggs and vegetables on tomato flavoured bread. Guests are welcomed by Sara Ford, known as Señora Ariola. If you are lucky you might get a table in the kitchen, reserved for special guests.

Horcher ★

Alfonso XII-6
Tel: 91 522 0731 Fax: 91 523 3490
(Closed Saturday lunch & Sunday)

The third generation of the Horcher family with its Germanic roots are now in charge. The restaurant is situated in a luxurious mansion on the edge of the Retiro Park and keeps up a high standard of both food and service. The cooking is in the hands of Gustavo "Moppy" Horcher and can best be characterised as central European haute cuisine. Game is a speciality in season. Look for venison, wild duck and boar. For dessert there are more central European dishes such as pancakes and strudels. If you arrive by car there is valet parking available.

Jockey ★★

Amador de los Rios 6
Tel: 91 319 2435 Fax: 91 319 2435
(Closed Saturday lunch, Sunday & August)

The gastronomic standard of Madrid's leading restaurants is very high and Jockey is very much a part of this group. Located in a quiet residential area, this is a classic restaurant much appreciated and frequented by leading business people in Madrid. It opened some 56 years ago and was restored and updated a few years ago. It has a special club-like atmosphere with equestrian paintings and bronzes, mahogany walls and racing-green banquettes. The restaurant manager, Carmelo Perez, winner of the national gastronomy prize, supervises a large and efficient staff. The cooking is very much devoted to Madrilino dishes with a good degustation menu. When I eat with friends in Madrid we tend to go to Jockey.

Principe de Viana ★

Manuel de Falla 5
Tel: 91 457 15 49 Fax: 91 457 52 83
(Closed Saturday lunch, Sunday & August)
Jesus Oyarbide and his son Javier who run this first class restaurant specialise in traditional Basque and Navarra cooking (Navarra is the province adjoining the Basque country and the Pyranees). Oyarbide was the first restaurateur to introduce this type of cuisine in Madrid. The service is mostly by waitresses dressed in traditional apron dresses and ruffled collars. As always in Spain, fish courses tend to dominate the menu and here are a couple of good choices: salt cod with garlic and monkfish with a wine and olive emulsion. The wine cellar is very good with Spanish Rioja wines being a particular strength.

Zalacain ★★1/2

Alvarez de Baena 4
Tel: 91 561 4840 Fax: 91 561 4732
(Closed Saturday lunch, Sunday & August)
Zalacain could be an exclusive villa in a quiet residential area but it is a famous restaurant with a great reputation. On my visits to Madrid I make sure I have at least one meal at this luxurious place with its deep apricot colour scheme, large tables, comfortable seating and attentive service. Chef Benjamin Urdiain offers a part Basque, part haute cuisine menu with dishes of great interest. Try oysters in port wine, langoustines with artichoke, turbot with cêpes and pigs' trotters stuffed with lamb. Excellent wine list.

Barcelona

Can Gaig ★

Passeig de Maragall 402
Tel: 93 429 1017 Fax: 93 429 7002
(Closed Sunday dinner & Monday)
Carles Gaig is the fourth generation chef/proprietor of this 130 year old family restaurant with high quality cuisine. It is a stylish establishment with good décor in warm colours and with plenty of fresh flowers. The cooking is of course based on Catalan dishes, both traditional and creative. Among the many interesting offerings on the menu are crème Catalan and Bresse chicken with pine-nuts and prunes. A good game dish is roast partridge with Iberian bacon. Do make a reservation.

La Dama ★

Avenida Diagonal 423

Tel: 93 202 0686 Fax: 93 200 7299

On one of the main boulevards we find this very stylish restaurant in a detached Catalan Art Nouveau building, from the beginning of the last century, designed by Manuel Sayrach. The four dining rooms are connected by a hand carved staircase and there are columns, old glass and sculptures that contribute to the atmosphere. The cooking is Catalan/French with dishes like aubergines stuffed with mushrooms and summer truffles, fillets of sole with king prawns and tarragon or baked duck fillets with peaches. This well located restaurant is a good place to entertain. My wife and I went there with a group of friends and thoroughly enjoyed it.

Neichel ★★

Beltran I Rózpide 16 bis

Tel: 93 203 8408 Fax: 93 205 6369

(Closed Saturday lunch & Sunday)

Barcelona and the Catalan region is known for its good food and excellent restaurants. One of the very best restaurants in Barcelona is Neichel. Surprisingly Jean-Louis Neichel is from Alsace, probably the only leading French chef cooking in Spain. He trained with the famous Alain Chapel near Lyon and came to Barcelona and opened Neichel in 1981. It is an elegant, spacious establishment, charmingly decorated and with a garden with lemon trees. Madame Emily Neichel is in charge of the dining room and will propose several menus, for example a six-course gourmet menu with small courses. On my last visit I sampled carpaccio of salmon and sea bass followed by honey-roasted duck with citrus fruits and ended with a gratin of rhubarb and strawberries with spicy ice-cream. Sommelier Xavier Petrirena will offer a large selection of Armagnacs.

Via Veneto ★1/2

Ganduxer 10-12

Tel: 93 200 7244 Fax: 93 201 6095

(Closed Saturday lunch, Sunday & 3 weeks in August)

Situated in a smart residential district this Belle Epoque style restaurant is one of the most exclusive in Barcelona. The cooking is Catalan with a French influence. I have always enjoyed being able to dine here in attractive surrroundings and with good food cooked by chef José Muniesa. He changes the menu daily using only the freshest produce from the local market. Some examples from

the menu are steamed lobster and its roe with mango in vanilla oil, baked hake cutlet with clams and spinach in green sauce or roast fillet of beef with five peppers and fettuccini. Try honey-caramelised apple with custard and saffron ice-cream or chocolate soufflé for dessert.

Near Barcelona

El Raco de Can Fabes ★★★

Sant Joan 6, San Celoni
Tel: 93 867 2851 Fax: 93 867 3861
(Closed Sunday dinner, Monday & 3 weeks in June/July)
Some things are too good to be missed. Half an hour (45 km) north west of Barcelona, in the little town of San Celoni, chef/patron Santi Santamaria turns out some remarkable dishes. I rank Santamaria one of the four top chefs in Spain and look forward to my next visit. Santamaria was born in this building in a quiet side street and it is not that easy to find. When you arrive you can watch the chefs at work and plan your gourmet meal. The cuisine is predominately Mediterranean which can be best tried by ordering the menu de degustation.

Cala Montjoi

El Bulli ★★★

Apartado 30
Tel: 972 15 0457 Fax: 972 15 0717
(only open March - September)
This is a very special place! International gastronomes from many parts of Europe travel here to enjoy Ferran Adria's extraordinary cooking. You have to book at least two months ahead to get a table as they are only open for dinner Tuesday through Sunday from March to September; but do check for last minute cancellations. Sometime ago I took a group of friends from England here for a very special meal. When I asked Ferran to propose a menu he replied: 'I want you to try a selection of all my current dishes' - and so we did, all 16 of them in a meal lasting four hours. That is real Spanish style! El Bulli is situated in a beautiful bay surrounded by gardens on the shores of the Mediterranean. It is approached by a narrow mountain road from the little town of Roses. There is no major town nearby so you either go north from Barcelona (100 miles / 165 kms) or south from Perpignan in France, which is what I recommend. It is worth the journey to enjoy the highly unusual and creative cooking of Ferran Adria, whom I consider to be one of Europe's greatest chefs.

Lasarte

Martín Berasategui ★★★

Loidi Kalea 4
Tel: 943 36 6471 Fax: 943 36 6107
(Closed Saturday lunch, Sunday dinner, Monday, mid December - mid January)

It is perhaps not realised in other countries that Basque cuisine is at the top of the gastronomic pyramid in Spain. Near and in San Sebastian are four of the finest restaurants in Spain. Martin Berasategui in Lasarte, 10 kms from San Sebastian, is definitely a three star restaurant in the Florman Guide although the Red Guide limits him to two. Martin is youngish and very creative and , as he says himself 'I am a chef of the market - everything I use is fresh and from the surrounding gardens and countryside'. Having first worked for his mother in a popular restaurant in San Sebastian he moved out 10 years ago and opened in a restored residence in the heart of the countryside. Among Martin's specialities are pastry and he is probably the best Basque pastry cook. A sample of his dishes is millefeuille of eel and foie gras and also gambas with onion ravioli. I would advise visitors to order the menu de dégustation to get a full sampling of Martin's talents.

Marbella

La Hacienda FF

salida Las Chapas
Tel: 95 283 1267 Fax: 95 283 3328
(Closed Monday, Tuesday & 4 weeks in November/December)

Here is my favourite restaurant in the Marbella area. It is nice to get away from the busy town and beach areas and drive up to the hills. La Hacienda is situated 12 kms away from Marbella on the high slopes with a wonderful view of the mountains in the north and the whole bay of Marbella. The restaurant is surrounded by tropical gardens. My wife and I have driven up many times and dined on the vast Andalusian style terrace. Signora Theresa Schiff is the owner and her daughter Cati and Francisco Galvez run the kitchen and produce some fine dishes. Among these are: strudel of lobster with vegetables in oregano, beef filet with rosemary and chocolate sauce (!) and a flan of fruit with a mint sauce.

Oyarzun

Zuberoa ★★

Barrio Iturriotz 8

Tel: 943 49 1228 Fax: 943 49 2679

(Closed Sunday dinner & Monday)

The Basque country is rich in starred restaurants. Zuberoa in Oyarzun is a near neighbour (11 kms) of San Sebastian in a lovely century-old country house, the oldest house in the whole of the Oyarzun valley. Chef/proprietor Hilario Abelaitz is a great chef who believes in the tradition of Basque cuisine but also in modern versions of traditional dishes. He has been enriching and refining his cooking for almost two decades. Among his specialities are foie gras in chick pea soup with fried bread, lobster in cinnamon oil, and supreme of pigeon with potato purée. To end the meal why not have coconut and bitter orange cream with almond brioche and chocolate sauce. There is also a menu de degustation.

San Pol de Mar

Sant Pau ★★

Nou 10

Tel: 93 760 06 62 Fax: 93 760 09 50

(Closed Sunday dinner, Monday & 3 weeks in November)

If you feel like a gourmet excursion north along the coast from Barcelona take a 40 minute train ride to San Pol de Mar. The train will drop you at the door of Carmen Ruscalleda's and Toni Balam's restaurant, Sant Pau. You are now in one of the best restaurants on the coast and Carmen will perhaps suggest her tasting menu. The regular menu will feature dishes like red mullet with black olives or sea bass on a bed of baby leeks in a sauce of sweet Catalan wine. An unusual meat dish is wild boar sausage with stewed pineapple and peach. The wine list has many fine Spanish wines. The restaurant is situated in an old house with a pleasant garden overlooking the sea.

San Sebastian

Arzak ★★★

Alto de Miracruz 21
Tel: 943 27 84 65 Fax: 943 27 27 53
(Closed Sunday dinner, Monday, 3 weeks June/July, 3 weeks November)

The Basque part of Spain is home to some of the finest chefs in the country. San Sebastian and the surrounding area is where four of them can be found, all reviewed in this guide. The best known and the only one right in San Sebastian itself is Arzak, away from the port and in the high part of the town. Opened in 1897 this comfortably furnished family inn has a lot of ambience. There is no chef more famous in Spain then Juan -Mari Arzak. Nowadays, assisted by his attractive daughter Eléna, he produces some exquisite dishes such as sautéed langoustines with spider crab meat and roast pigeon with coriander and cumin served in its juice. For dessert I can mention an orange croquante with a tarragon flavoured pear sorbet - a surprising but excellent dish. We drove to San Sebastian specifically to visit Arzak and received a warm welcome. The cuisine is predominately Basque with Spanish variations.

Akelare ★★

Paseo del Padre Orcolaga 56
Tel: 943 21 20 52 Fax: 943 21 92 68
(Closed Sunday dinner, Monday & February)

A few kilometres outside San Sebastian, on the slopes of Monte Igueldo, this restaurant offers you a spectacular view of both the sea and the town of San Sebastian below. Owner/chef Pedro Subijana grows his own vegetables and aromatic herbs for his guests to enjoy. The food is spectacular too as Subijana is one of the pioneers of modern Basque cuisine. Looking at the menu we find: filet of salmon with risotto, langoustines with fresh pasta, sea bass with green pepper and squid in a sauce of its own ink. For dessert try chocolate & rhubarb ganache.

Sweden (+46)

Stockholm

Bon Lloc ★1/2

Regeringsgatan 111

Tel: 08 660 6060 Fax: 08 10 76 35

(Closed Sunday & mid-July - mid-August)

The most important cookery competition in the world is Bocuse d'Or, started and led by Paul Bocuse. To win a Bocuse medal is a great honour for a chef. Mathias Dahlgren, chef at Bon Lloc, won a gold medal in the Bocuse d'Or in 1997. He has also moved this restaurant to more spacious premises in the centre of town. As the name indicates there are Spanish/Catalan connections and the cooking is Nordic Mediterranean of a high standard. I recently lunched here with a group of friends and we enjoyed these dishes: tuna carpaccio Niçoise, chanterel chicken with duck liver cappuccino, red wine poached figs with roasted nut bread and finally hazelnut soufflé with vanilla ice-cream. An excellent meal!

Edsbacka Krog ★★

Sollentunavägen 220, Sollentuna

Tel: 08 96 33 00 Fax: 08 96 40 19

(Closed Sunday & 3 weeks in July)

The history of this famous inn north of Stockholm goes back to 1626 when it obtained Royal privilege to serve beer, wine and food to travellers. The Royal charter can be found on the wall of the entrance. The old inn closed in the last century but the building was modernised and re-opened as a restaurant in 1983. Today Edsbacka is rated one of the very best restaurants in Sweden thanks to chef/patron Christer Lingström. It is very popular to make an excursion from Stockholm to Sollentuna (15 km) to enjoy a relaxed meal in this country restaurant. Recently I was privileged to be part of a group of gastronomes who dined at Edsbacka with the King and Queen of Sweden. They are both very interested in food and the King is actually an active member of the Swedish Gastronomic Academy. On this occasion we ate terrine de truite saumonée followed by morue fraîche (cod) et coquille Saint Jacques grillées, selle d'agneau and as a dessert crème à vanille sous gélée à la rhubarbe. A good meal although a couple of courses lacked real edge. Incidentally the cover of this guide book was photographed at Edsbacka.

Erik's Bakficka

FF

Frederikhovsgatan 4
Tel: 08 660 1599 Fax: 08 663 2567
(Closed Saturday lunch, Sunday & 3 weeks in July/August)

There is always a demand for a friendly, relaxed place with good food at reasonable prices. Erik's Bakficka fits the bill perfectly. Erik is my long time friend Erik Lallerstedt, one of Sweden's best known and respected chefs (he also owns Gondolen, see 'Also recommended'). Bakficka translates into "back pocket" in English and means that it is a neighbourhood place as familiar to you as your own back pocket. Erik's is located in the most fashionable residential area of Stockholm, but not far from the centre.

Franska Matsalen

★★

At the Grand Hotel
Tel: 08 679 3584 Fax: 08 611 8686
(Dinner only, closed Saturday & Sunday)

Grand is the number one luxury hotel in Sweden and I would certainly recommend any visitor to Stockholm to book in there. Many of the rooms overlook the water with magnificent views of the historic old town and the Royal palace. The hotel has two dining rooms but the main one which I will mention here is the Franska Matsalen (the French Dining Room). Open only in the evening, under the direction of Roland Persson, it has an excellent selection of classic dishes.

Lisa Elmquist and Gerda Johansson

FF

Östermalms Saluhall, Östermalms Torg
Tel: 08 55 34 04 10 (Lisa) & Tel: 08 55 34 04 40 (Gerda)
(Lunch only)

In Stockholm one can find one of the finest indoor food markets anywhere. Some 25 merchants have top class fish, meat, fruit, vegetables, bread, pastries and so on for sale. And then there is Lisa and Gerda: these are two small restaurants side by side and part of two fish merchants. They stay open all day for a light meal but close in the evening when the market closes. This is not the place for a business lunch as the noise level is high but the whole market has a terrific atmosphere. May I be immodest and mention that my maternal grandfather and great grandfather were two Swedish bankers who took the initiative to plan and build this famous market hall.

Operakällaren ★★

Operahuset, Karl X11's Torg
Tel: 08 676 5801 Fax: 08 676 5872
(Dinner only & Closed July)

There is no more magnificent restaurant in Scandinavia than Operakällaren. Literally translated the name means the 'cellar of the opera' but it is not a cellar at all, it is simply the rear section of the opera house. It has a magnificent location on the water facing the royal palace. Sweden's most famous chef and restaurateur Tore Wretman modernised and re-opened this establishment some thirty years ago. The head chef is Swiss born Werner Vögeli who is also the Scandinavian representative of Bocuse d'Or. The chef, Italian born Stefano Catenacci, is in charge of the Operakëllaren dining room. It has recently begun to serve more French food and has reached high standards at the very top in Sweden, which is why I am now awarding them two stars. The dining room and its verandah by the water is extremely elegant. Should you wish to eat a lighter and simpler meal there are two other restaurants, part of the same establishment, Café Opera and the Opera Bar. All I can say is don't miss it.

Paul & Norbert ★

Strandvägen 9
Tel: 08 663 8183 Fax: 08 661 7236
(Closed Saturday, Sunday & Monday)

In several ways Paul and Norbert is different from other top Stockholm eating-places. First the chef, Norbert Lang, is German, although a long time resident of Sweden. Secondly it is very small with only nine tables. It is on fashionable Strandvägen which is reflected in the rather high prices. The menu is very varied with some interesting soups. I really like the oyster bisque with a spoonful of caviar on the side. A particularly good dish is his goose liver terrine - either with mushrooms or chestnuts. Make sure to reserve a table.

Pontus in the Greenhouse ★1/2

Österlånggatan 17
Tel: 08 23 85 00 Fax: 08 796 6069
(Closed Sunday)

No restaurant in Stockholm has a more original menu than Pontus. Young chef Pontus Frithiof has the capacity and the imagination to create dishes that raise eyebrows. When I was last there with some friends we chose a tasting menu

called Pontus Temptation which consists of eight courses and also an amuse bouche and a pre-dessert. This menu is varied quite often so you can go back and have many new selections. The menu is also available with a different well-chosen glass of wine with each dish. I urge my readers to try it. The Greenhouse is to be found in the middle of the old town within walking distance of the Royal Palace.

Wedholms Fisk ★★

Nybrokajen 17
Tel: 08 611 7874 Fax: 08 678 6011
(Closed Saturday lunch & Sunday)
The Swedes love fish and shellfish and many chefs are very good at preparing it, but best of all is Bengt Wedholm. He and I have been friends for more years than I can remember and the first thing I do when arriving in Stockholm is to head for Wedholms Fisk. It has a fairly simple one star interior but the cooking is of the highest standard and I have no hesitation in awarding Bengt two stars. Recently a visitor from the USA asked me to choose a seafood restaurant for an important lunch he was giving in Stockholm and naturally I chose Wedholms. I was among the guests and enjoyed tartar of salmon and salmon roe with crème fraiche and fricasée of sole, turbot, lobster and scallops with champagne sauce.

Also recommended:

Den Gyldene Freden O

Osterlånggatan 51
Tel: 08 24 97 60 Fax: 08 21 38 70
An historic vaulted 18th century cellar where chef Ulf Kappen presents quality Swedish home cooking.

Gondolen O

Stadsgården 6
Tel: 08 641 70 90 Fax: 08 641 11 40
What a view! A glass enclosed gondola supported in the air, serving good food.

Fredsgatan 12 ★

Fredsgatan 12
Tel: 08 24 80 52 Fax: 08 411 73 48
Imaginative cooking and unusual presentation by chef Melker Andersson. Full review in next year's edition.

Teatergrillen FF

Nybrogatan 3
Tel: 08 679 6842 Fax: 08 611 3206
Perfect for light business lunches (a favourite of my son's) but the alcoves are also right for intimate dinners. High standard of food and service.

Gothenburg

Sjömagasinet ★★

Klippans Kulturreservat 5
Tel: 031 775 5920 Fax: 031 24 55 39
(Closed Saturday lunch)
Fish and shellfish is the order of the day here. Not surprisingly since this restaurant is set by the water in a converted warehouse next to the fishing harbour where you have a fine view of passing ships as you eat. Chef/proprietor Leif Mannerström is an old friend of mine who has a great reputation as the leading chef in Gothenburg and western Sweden. One of his specialities is to serve the Swedish golden caviar - löjrom - usually on toast. These fish eggs are only found in Swedish and Finnish waters and are a great delicacy. In English the name is bleak roe and in French, oeufs d'ablettes. If you are a visitor to Sweden this is a must as a starter. In summertime meals are served on the terrace where there is also a shellfish bar.

Fiskekrogen ★

Lilla Torget 1
Tel: 031 10 10 05 Fax: 031 10 10 06
(Closed Sunday, & 3 weeks July/August)
Not surprisingly the name of this restaurant in English is the Fish Restaurant, and what better place for such a restaurant to be than in Gothenburg, the main fishing port of Sweden. Owner Lars Ahlström runs a restaurant with a very large choice of seafood. I would resommend that you start with a plateau of shellfish or a carpaccio of tuna and as a main course have grilled turbot with a crispy skin. There are also very good desserts The wine list is French dominated, especially with some good Burgundies.

28+ ★

Götabergsgatan 28
Tel: 031 20 21 61 Fax: 031 81 97 57
(Closed Sunday & July)

A cellar restaurant with a cheese shop at the entrance is the setting for this gourmet restaurant, one of the best in western Sweden. The cheese selection is of course excellent but before we reach that stage here are some of the dishes that should be considered. Start perhaps with grilled scall-lops and a truffle risotto. Move on to braised filet of sole. During the game season you can try pheasant, both roasted and confit, or any other Swedish game - there is a big choi-ce of game in Sweden. The wine list is substantial with a large choice to match your cheese. Ulf Johanson was recently named the Chef of the Year in Sweden.

Also recommended:

Steak FF

Arkivgatan 7
Tel: 031 18 50 15 Fax: 031 778 38 85

Leif Mannerström has created a unique and excellent meat restaurant. Drinks are around a long table by the meat counter.

Malmö

Petri Pumpa ★

Norra Vallgatan 62
Tel: 040 664 48 80 Fax: 040 664 48 50

Possibly the best food in Skåne. Recently installed in the first class Savoy Hotel.

Switzerland (+41)

Bern

Schultheissenstube O

Hôtel Schweizerhof, Bahnhofplatz 11
Tel: 031 326 8080 Fax: 031 326 8090
(Closed Sunday & 3 weeks in July)

Although Bern is the capital of Switzerland there are no star restaurants around. My choice in Bern is the Schultheissenstube on the first floor of the excellent Hotel Schweizerhof facing the central railway station. Chef Daniel Krebs is very creative and on the menu we find interesting dishes such as tartare of turbot sweet and sour with or without caviar. There is also filet of lemon sole with leeks. In season there is also excellent game and foie gras.

Basel

Bruderholz ★★

Bruderholzallee 42
Tel: 061 361 8222 Fax: 061 361 8203
(Closed Sunday & Monday)

There are so many good restaurants all over Switzerland that sometimes the choice can be difficult, but less so in Basel where I warmly recommend Bruderholz. Situated in a 1920's villa on a residential hillside overlooking the town the restaurant has three dining rooms but you can also eat in the garden in summertime which I did on my last visit. The late, great Hans Stucki was the chef/patron for some 38 years and established high standards of cooking and service. His successors are Pierre Buess (owner) and Jean-Claude Wicky (head chef) and they keep up the tradition and present some very good dishes such as fricassée of langoustines with curry and a duck nantais with vinegar and honey; and why not end with a soufflé with a fruit sauce. To accompany this I recommend some of the excellent Swiss white wines featured on the list. Please note that there is a lunch menu for only 68 Swiss Francs.

Geneva

Auberge du Lion D'Or ★

5 place Pierre-Gautier, Cologny
Tel: 022 736 4432 Fax: 022 786 7462
(Closed Saturday & Sunday)

Cologny is on a hill outside Geneva, only 3-4 miles out of town, on the road to Evian. At the Auberge Lion d'Or you will have a beautiful view over the town and Lake Geneva through the large windows in the restaurant. In good weather you can eat outside in the garden, as we did last summer. The Auberge has a reputation for good food, provided by Gilles Dupont and Irishman Thomas Byrne, joint chefs de cuisine. The main restaurant offers dishes such as marbré du foie gras aux aubergines et cacao. If you wish to eat a simpler meal there is also Le Bistro de Cologny in the same building, and served by the same kitchen.

Le Béarn ★★

4 quai de la Poste
Tel: 022 321 0028 Fax: 022 781 3115
(Closed Sunday)

'Traditional' is an important word when describing this Geneva landmark. Traditional, high quality French cuisine is what is on offer in a small restaurant attractively located by the river Rhone. Jean Paul Goddard, chef/patron, and his wife Denise will look after you with care in their two dining rooms with very different décor; one elegant, one rustic. I have enjoyed many a good meal here. Let me mention a few dishes: green asparagus flan with morels, and a good fish course is sea bass Provençale on a bed of vegetables. I have also tried filet mignon de veau moutardé (with mustard) and fresh herbs. The wine list has many interesting wines from the Geneva region, complementing the French wines. Service is good and there is an inexpensive lunch menu.

Le Chat Botté ★

Hôtel Beau Rivage, 13 quai du Mont-Blanc
Tel: 022 716 6920 Fax: 022 716 6060

Beau Rivage is one of Geneva's smaller luxury hotels on the quai facing the lake and the famous water jet. In good weather the Chat Botté (puss-in-boots!) moves out on to a rather noisy terrace where my wife and I lunched a few months ago. Some Geneva friends of mine think of this place as the best in town but my last meal was not quite up to scratch. It may have been a one-off. Chef Richard Cressac creates dishes such as coquille St Jacques poêlées

sauce aux épices or émincés de rognon avec moutarde a l'áncienne. If you would like a complete change of cuisine there is another restaurant in the hotel, Le Patara, serving Thai cuisine.

Le Neptune ★1/2

Hôtel Mandarin Oriental du Rhône, 1 quai Turrettini
Tel: 022 909 0006 Fax: 022 909 0010
(Closed Saturday, Sunday & 3 weeks in August)

As the name and location imply, Neptune is a seafood restaurant right on the banks of Lake Geneva in the luxury Hotel du Rhône. On my visits to Geneva I try to fit in a meal here as I particularly like seafood and have found some good dishes prepared by young chef Eric Gascon. Try the roasted lobster tails with caramelised salsify or turbot with onions and feta cheese. There are several interesting fish varieties that can be taken out of Lake Geneva and you might well find them on the menu when you visit.

Also recommended:

Le Cygne ★

The Noga Hilton, 19 quai du Mont Blanc
Tel: 022 908 9085 Fax: 022 908 9090

A very good location at the top of the hotel with a fine view over the lake and the Alps. Sophisticated, well presented menu.

Roberto O

10 rue Pierre-Fatio
Tel: 022 311 8033 Fax: 022 311 84 66

Roberto is the best Italian restaurant in town, with good service and fairly moderate prices.

Lausanne

Hôtel de Ville ★★★

1 rue d'Yverdon, Crissier
Tel: 021 634 0505 Fax: 021 634 2464
(Closed 3 weeks July/August)

For many years I have considered the Hotel de Ville as one of the best (possibly the best) restaurants I have ever eaten in. I know what I am talking about as I have been there over 50 times in the last 25 years. Its reputation was first established by the legendary Fredy Girardet. When he retired four years ago his long time chef de cuisine Philippe Rochat took over and I am happy to report that standards

are as high as ever. Madame Rochat is not only a charming hostess but has also won the New York marathon! The reputation of Philippe Rochat is so high that you are advised to book a long time ahead for dinner. Restaurant Manager Louis Villeneuve is by many considered to be the finest manager in the business. When selecting from the menu do follow his advice. I usually eat the menu de degustation, with some 8 or 9 dishes in small portions. From the menu try timbale de chanterelles à la fricassée de ris de veau au fumet de sous-bois, suprêmes de rouget de roche croustillants and canette sauvagine. My absolute favourite dessert is passion fruit soufflé. This restaurant is a must!

A Personal Tribute to Fredy Girardet...

Over the years I have got to know, and made friends with many great chefs but none greater than Fredy Girardet in Crissier, Switzerland. His greatness is well recognised within the fraternity of chefs. The French Gault-Millau guide gave him their maximum 19 points, already in 1976, and he kept it until he retired in 1997 at the age of 60. Girardet is the only chef to have been given three stars by Michelin on his first appearance in their guide.

I first discovered Fredy in March 1976 when I dined in his restaurant in Crissier. I have since returned regularly and enjoyed more than 50 meals over a 25 year period - and I have kept the menus.

One of the secrets of Girardet's success is that he was always in the kitchen personally leading his 20-strong brigade. He did not open other restaurants or cook away from Crissier, he was always at the stoves running a silent kitchen - most unusual. In retirement Girardet has recently published a superb cookery book which I am now enjoying reading. I wish him all the best.

Also recommended:

La Grappe d'Or ★

3 Cheneau de Bourg

Tel: 021 323 0760 Fax: 021 323 2230

Excellent restaurant in Lausanne with cooking by Peter Baermann. Wonderful desserts and a great wine list.

Montreux

Le Pont de Brent ★★★

à Brent
Tel: 021 964 5230 Fax: 021 964 5530
(Closed Sunday & Monday)

On the hills above Montreaux, only 4km up from the town is a small but superb gastronomic haven. The restaurant is not large but well decorated and outside is a pleasant garden where you can take a drink in clement weather. Gerard Rabaey, the patron, is a modest but very talented chef who has come to be recognised as one of the best. He does not seek publicity but just gets on with creating lovely dishes. A few of the delicacies you can order are rouget (red mullet) in various ways, lapin (rabbit) with basilic. I remember having veal kidneys with juniper sauce and ending with a hot soufflé with berries. Don't miss this gem!

Verbier

Roland Pierroz ★

Hotel Rosalp, Rue de Médran
Tel: 027 771 63 23 Fax: 027 771 10 59
(Closed May, June, October, November)

Gourmet food in the mountains? Why not? In the always fashionable ski resort of Verbier you will find one of the best restaurants in Switzerland in the hands of bearded chef/patron Roland Pierroz. He is also the vice-president of Les Grandes Tables de Suisse. I happen to be an active skier and have skied many times in Verbier, often ending the day with a dinner at this restaurant. I have also stayed in the Hotel Rosalp which houses the restaurant and is in the very centre of the village. There is a more informal restaurant in the same building called La Pinte. It is remarkable how Pierroz has overcome transport problems to provide quality food at such a high altitude. On the menu is langoustine with a sauce of yellow tomatoes and courgette flowers and as a main course lamb from Sisteron.

Vufflens-le-Château

L'Ermitage ★★★

Tel: 021 804 6868 Fax: 021 802 2240
(Closed Sunday, Monday & 3 weeks in August)

A good meal brings its own pleasures but if taken in attractive surroundings so much the better. Bernard and Ruth Ravet's restaurant, in an old winery surrounded by gardens with a lake, is a lovely place to visit. There are also nine bedrooms should you like to stay overnight. The

vineyards are not far away. Bernard is a very respected French-born chef and is considered among the best in Switzerland. If the weather is good you can take your aperitifs and amuse bouche in the garden. Sitting down for dinner in the restaurant you might consider trying a slowly smoked salmon, one of many delicacies from the restaurant's own smoke-house, or try omble chevalier (Arctic char) and then perhaps duckling roasted on a spit. Fresh bread is baked on the premises every day. After a couple of miniature pre-desserts you could have peach tart tatin with iced pine kernel parfait.

Zurich

Baur Au Lac ★

Talstrasse 1

Tel: 01 220 5020 Fax: 01 220 5044

This hotel is a prestigious landmark in Zurich, superbly located on the shore of Lake Zurich and at the beginning of the fashionable Bahnhofstrasse. The hotel has three excellent restaurants and, unusually, I am featuring all three in this review. The most luxurious is restaurant Le Français (only open October to May) then there is Le Pavillon, a summer restaurant set right by the river, and next to the hotel's private park, and finally there is Rive Gauche, which is more informal and my favourite. Whether you are doing business or shopping in Zurich, these three are a good starting point. In the bar there are over 100 malt whiskies to choose from.

Kronenhalle FF

Rämistrasse 4

Tel: 01 251 6669 Fax: 01 251 6681

Art and tradition - that is what Kronenhalle is about. Famous artists' paintings on the walls, both Chagall and Picasso as well as Bonnard and Klee and traditional food on the plates. In many ways Kronenhalle is typical of the German part of Switzerland and its substantial food. There are quite a number of regular guests so be sure to make a reservation. Don't miss the bar, which serves all the classic cocktails.

Petermanns Kunststuben ★★★

Seestrasse 160, Küsnacht
Tel: 01 910 0715 Fax: 01 910 0495
(Closed Sunday & Monday)

If you are in Zurich and want to sit down to one of the best meals available in that part of Switzerland it is worth taking yourself - and maybe a guest or two - to the little town of Küsnacht, only 8 kilometres (5 miles) away along the lake. It is my favourite restaurant in the whole of the German speaking section of Switzerland. Horst Petermann and his wife Iris will receive you in their flower-filled dining room overlooking the lake. You will see from the menu that there are many tempting dishes: you could start with foie gras with a coating of black truffle and a port wine sauce and then move on to a fillet of red mullet and stuffed calamari with sweet peppers. Another dish I have tried is Breton lobster in jelly. As always in Switzerland the wine list has very good Swiss white wines and many French wines.

Witschi's ★1/2

Zürcherstrasse 55
Tel: 01 750 4460 Fax: 01 750 1968
(Closed Sunday & Monday)

Situated in a small town, around ten kilometres north of Zurich, Witschi's restaurant makes a tempting destination for an excursion to have a first class meal. Heinz Witschi is one of the finest chefs in the German speaking part of Switzerland. The restaurant is attractive, with clay-tiled floors, pretty paintings on the walls and flower-pots. There is also a water fountain and you will be given a friendly welcome by Lydia, the head-waitress. Here is a selection of dishes to consider: asparagus charlotte with fresh morels in vinegar, filet of sander (perch-pike) with celery and garden vegetables and as a main course, tender lamb chops from best end of neck. For dessert I recommend a light lemon soufflé. The restaurant also has a pleasant terrace, and a private garage for customers.

Eastern Europe

Eastern Europe does not fall within the scope of this first edition of the Florman Guide, but maybe we will research and include these countries in future editions. For now, and to give some help to travellers here is a brief listing of good restaurants in five of the most important cities:

Czech Republic (+420)

Prague

Vinarna V Zátisi	Liliová 1, Betlémské Nám	Tel: 02 2222 1155
Hradcany	Keplerova Ul 6	Tel: 02 2430 2150
La Perle de Prague	Rasínovo Nábrezi	Tel: 02 2198 4160
Bellevue	Smetanovo Nábrezi 18	Tel: 02 2222 1438

Hungary (+36)

Budapest

Gundel	Allatkérti útca 2	Tel: 01 321 3550
Robinson	Városligeti tó	Tel: 01 343 3776
Mátyás Pince	Március 15 tér, no 7	Tel: 01 338 4711
Fausto's	Dohány útca 5	Tel: 01 269 6806
Vadrózsa	Pentelei Molnár útca 15	Tel: 01 326 5817

Poland (+48)

Warsaw

Malinowa	Krakowskie Przedmiescie	Tel: 022 551 1833
Casa Valdemar	Ul Pie kna 7-9	Tel: 022 628 8140
U Fukiera	Rynek Starego Miasta 27	Tel: 022 831 1013
Belvedere	Ul Agrykoli 1A	Tel: 022 841 4806

Russia (+7)

Moscow

Le Duc	2 1905 Goda Ulitsa	Tel: 095 2550390
Café Pushkin	26a Tverskoi Boulevard	Tel: 095 2295590
Mario	17 Klimashkina Ulitsa	Tel: 095 2536505
1 Red Square	1 Red Square	Tel: 095 9253600

St Petersburg

Noble Nest	21 Ulitsa Dekabristow	Tel: 812 3123205
The Taleon Club	59 Naberezhnaya Reki Moiki	Tel: 812 3157645

The Three Star Restaurants

Alain Chapel	Mionnay
L'Ambroisie	Paris
Al Sorriso	Soriso
Alain Ducasse	Paris
Antica Osteria del Ponte	Milan
Arpège	Paris
Arzak	San Sebastian
Auberge de l'Eridan (Marc Veyrat)	Annecy
Auberge de l'Ill	Illhaeusern
Boyer Les Crayères	Reims
Le Bristol	Paris
Bruneau	Brussels
Buerehiesel	Strasbourg
Comme Chez Soi	Brussels
Côte d'Or	Saulieu
Côte St Jacques	Joigny
Au Crocodile	Strasbourg
Dai Pescatore	Canneto sull' Oglio
De Karmeliet	Bruges
Dieter Müller	Bergisch Gladbach
Don Alfonso 1890	Sant Agata sui Due Golfi
El Bulli	Cala Montjoi
El Raco de Can Fabes	Near Barcelona
Enoteca Pinchiorri	Florence
L'Ermitage	Vufflens Le Chateau
L'Esperance	Vezelay
Heinz Winkler	Aschau im Chiemgau
Hotel de Ville (Philippe Rochat)	Lausanne
Le Gavroche	London
Georges Blanc	Vonnas
Gordon Ramsay	London
Grand Vefour	Paris
Im Schiffchen	Düsseldorf
Jardin de Sens	Montpellier
Lameloise	Chagny
Louis XV	Monte Carlo
Lucas Carton	Paris
Maison de Bricourt	Cancale
Martin Berasategui	Lasarte
Michel Bras	Laguiole
Paul Bocuse	Lyon
Petermann's Kunststuben	Zürich
Pierre Gagnaire	Paris
Le Pont de Brent	Montreux
Les Prés d'Eugenie (Michel Guerard)	Eugenie les Bains
Pyramide	Vienne
Schwarzwaldstube	Baiersbronn
Taillevent	Paris
La Tante Claire	London
La Tour d'Argent	Paris
Troisgros	Roanne
Waldhotel Sonnora	Wittlich
Waterside Inn	Bray-on-Thames

United States of America (+1)

Surely our readers travel to the USA now and then and would like to eat as well there as they do in Europe. Without going into detail the Florman Guide now offers a small selection of the best restaurants in the major city areas. Here are 26 top restaurants that I have chosen:

Atlanta

Ritz Carlton
181 Peachtree Street Tel: 404 659 0400

Seeger's
111 West Paces Ferry Road Tel: 404 846 9779

Boston

L'Espalier
30 Gloucester Street Tel: 617 262 3023

Chicago

Charlie Trotter's
816 West Armitage Avenue Tel: 773 248 6228

Le Français
Wheeling, 269 South Milwaukee Tel: 847 541 7470

Cincinnati

Maisonette
114 East 6th Street Tel: 513 721 2260

Dallas

The Mansion
2821 Turtle Creek Boulevard Tel: 214 559 2100

Detroit

The Lark
6430 Farmington, West Bloomfield Tel: 248 661 4466

Houston

Deville
Hotel Four Seasons, 1300 Lamar Street Tel: 713 650 1300

Los Angeles

Spago
176 N. Canon Drive, Beverly Hills Tel: 310 385 0880

Matsuhisa
129 North La Cienega Boulevard, Beverly Hills
Tel: 310 659 9639

L'Orangerie
903 North La Cienega Boulevard, West Hollywood
Tel: 310 652 9770

New Orleans
Emeril's
800 Tchoupitoulas Street Tel: 504 528 9393
Windsor Court
300 Gravier Street Tel: 504 523 6000

New York
Aureole
34 East 61st Street Tel: 212 319 1660
Le Bernardin
155 West 51st Street Tel: 212 489 1515
Le Cirque
455 Madison Avenue Tel: 212 303 7788
Daniel
60 East 65th Street Tel: 212 288 0033
La Grenouille
3 East 52nd Street Tel: 212 752 1495
Lutece
249 East 50th Street Tel: 212 752 2225

Philadelphia
Le Bec Fin
1523 Walnut Street Tel: 212 567 1000

San Francisco
Chez Panisse
1517 Shattuck Avenue, Berkeley Tel: 510 548 5525
La Folie
2316 Polk Street Tel: 415 776 5577

Napa Valley-north of San Francisco
French Laundry
6640 Washington Street, Yountville Tel: 707 944 2380

Washington D.C.
Citronelle
Hotel Latham, 3000 M Street Tel: 202 625 2150

Near Washington D.C.
The Inn at Little Washington
Middle & Main Streets, Gainsville Tel: 540 675 3800

Epilogue

When you reach this page and have tried some, if not all of the gastronomic temples and culinary Olympians recommmended in this book you can count yourself among the truly blessed.

Many of the great chefs of the world have been tested time and again by Charles Florman's sensitive palate and superb memory of special recipes and menus. His scrutiny and judgement is based upon a lifetime of good eating and his and his family's many visits to Europe's greatest restaurants. Who else can claim more than 50 visits at the wonderful tables of Fredy Girardet, in Crissier, considered by many the greatest chef of all!

His private list of the best has long been sought after by all who know of his quest for sampling epicurean delights. His decision to share it with us is a treat for all gastronomes and a blessing for chefs he has encountered. Where would they be without a good recommendation?

For the consummate gourmet, the pleasures of the table are the highlights of the day. Few can match Charles Florman's knowledge in selecting the best. Joining him in this pursuit has enriched my life and added to my mirth, as well as the girth.

If you have not already begun your culinary journey with Charles when reading this page go back to the beginning of the guide and start planning immediately. It will surprise and delight you with every new discovery.

To make sure you do not stray from the complete experience he has brought together the wisdom of other bon viveurs to guide us into the ultimate enjoyment of champagne, claret, cognac, cigars and truffles - all luxurious accoutrements for the total sybarite.

When Charles told me about his idea of sharing his experiences of writing a guide, I immediately ordered 300 copies before a single page was written to give to my friends. One of my best investments.

Anthelme Brillat-Savarin once said "the discovery of a new dish does more for the happiness of mankind than the dis-

covery of a star". To find that elusive dish you need to find the place where it was created. This guide will take you straight there. So go forth and enjoy it!

Some other thoughts for you to consider:

All human history attests...
That happiness for a man - the hungry sinner -
Since Eve ate apples, much depends on dinner!
Lord Byron

"*There is no love sincerer than the love of food*"
George Bernard Shaw

"*The Golden Rule when reading the menu in a restaurant is if you can't pronounce it, you can't afford it*"
Frank Muir

"*For myself the only immortality I desire is to invent a new sauce*"
Oscar Wilde

"*One cannot think well, love well, sleep well unless one has dined well*"
Virginia Woolf

"*Fish to taste right must swim three times, in water, in butter and in wine*"
Polish proverb

"*No man is lonely while eating spaghetti - it requires so much attention*"
Christopher Morley

"*Tell me what you eat and I will tell you who you are*"
Brillat-Savarin

Jan Staël von Holstein
World Traveller

VINTAGE WINE CHART

	1970	1971	1975	1978	1982	1983	1985	1986	1988	1989	1990	1991	1992	1993	1994	1995	1996	1997	1998	1999	2000
Bordeaux R	6^{Δ}	4^{Δ}	5^{Δ}	5^{Δ}	$7^{\dagger}$	5^{Δ}	$6^{\dagger}$	$5^{\dagger}$	$5^{\dagger}$	$6^{\dagger}$	7*	2^{Δ}	2^{Δ}	3^{Δ}	3^{Δ}	6*	5*	3*	5*	4*	6*
Sauternes W	5^{Δ}	6^{Δ}	6^{Δ}	3^{Δ}	4^{Δ}	$6^{\dagger}$	$4^{\dagger}$	$5^{\dagger}$	$7^{\dagger}$	$7^{\dagger}$	$7^{\dagger}$	-	-	-	2^{Δ}	$4^{\dagger}$	5*	6*	5*	6*	4*
Burgundy R	5^{Δ}	6^{Δ}	-	7^{Δ}	4^{Δ}	4^{Δ}	6^{Δ}	3^{Δ}	$6^{\dagger}$	$6^{\dagger}$	7*	5^{Δ}	3^{Δ}	6*	3^{Δ}	5*	7*	4*	5*	6*	5*
Burgundy W	-	6^{Δ}	-	6^{Δ}	4^{Δ}	4^{Δ}	7^{Δ}	5^{Δ}	4^{Δ}	$7^{\dagger}$	6^{Δ}	3^{Δ}	6^{Δ}	$5^{\dagger}$	3^{Δ}	$7^{\dagger}$	6*	$6^{\dagger}$	5*	4*	5*
Rhône R	-	5^{Δ}	-	$7^{\dagger}$	5^{Δ}	$6^{\dagger}$	$6^{\dagger}$	3^{Δ}	$6^{\dagger}$	$6^{\dagger}$	7*	3^{Δ}	$4^{\dagger}$	3^{Δ}	$5^{\dagger}$	6*	$4^{\dagger}$	$3^{\dagger}$	7*	6*	5*
Rhine & Alsace W	-	7^{Δ}	6^{Δ}	-	4^{Δ}	6^{Δ}	6^{Δ}	4^{Δ}	5^{Δ}	$7^{\dagger}$	$7^{\dagger}$	4^{Δ}	5^{Δ}	5^{Δ}	5^{Δ}	6*	$6^{\dagger}$	6*	5*	6*	5*
Italy (Piedmont) R	6^{Δ}	7^{Δ}	3^{Δ}	6^{Δ}	6^{Δ}	5^{Δ}	$7^{\dagger}$	6^{Δ}	$6^{\dagger}$	$7^{\dagger}$	$7^{\dagger}$	$5^{\dagger}$	3^{Δ}	$5^{\dagger}$	$4^{\dagger}$	5*	6*	6*	6*	7*	5*

Italy (Tuscany) R	7^Δ	6^Δ	5^Δ	6^Δ	5^Δ	6^Δ	7^Δ	4^Δ	6^Δ	3^Δ	$7^\dagger$	$6^\dagger$	1^Δ	$5^\dagger$	$4^\dagger$	5*	5*	6*	5*	6*	4*
Spain (Rioja) R	5^Δ	-	5^Δ	4^Δ	7^Δ	4^Δ	$6^\dagger$	3^Δ	$4^\dagger$	$6^\dagger$	$5^\dagger$	$3^\dagger$	4^Δ	3^Δ	$6^\dagger$	$7^\dagger$	5*	5*	4*	5*	4*
California R	7^Δ	-	3^Δ	7^Δ	2^Δ	2^Δ	4^Δ	5^Δ	3^Δ	4^Δ	6^Δ	6^Δ	$6^\dagger$	$5^\dagger$	$7^\dagger$	$6^\dagger$	5*	6*	4*	5*	4*
Chile R	-	-	-	-	-	-	-	-	-	-	6^Δ	4^Δ	4^Δ	$6^\dagger$	$4^\dagger$	$7^\dagger$	$5^\dagger$	$6^\dagger$	5*	7*	5*
Australia (NSW) R	7^Δ	2^Δ	6^Δ	3^Δ	5^Δ	6^Δ	4^Δ	5^Δ	4^Δ	6^Δ	3^Δ	$7^\dagger$	4^Δ	$6^\dagger$	$5^\dagger$	$6^\dagger$	$4^\dagger$	5*	7*	5*	7*
Australia (South) R	5^Δ	6^Δ	6^Δ	6^Δ	7^Δ	3^Δ	6^Δ	$7^\dagger$	$6^\dagger$	3^Δ	$7^\dagger$	$7^\dagger$	4^Δ	4^Δ	$6^\dagger$	3^Δ	$7^\dagger$	$5^\dagger$	7*	5*	5*

Good vintages not shown: Champagne: 70^Δ, 71^Δ, $\underline{75}^\Delta$, 76^Δ, 79^Δ, $\underline{82}^\dagger$, $\underline{85}^\dagger$, 89^Δ, $\underline{90}^\dagger$, $\underline{96}$* California: $\underline{74}^\Delta$, $87^\dagger$

Sauternes: $\underline{67}^\Delta$ Rhône: $\underline{72}^\Delta$ Port: 60^Δ, $\underline{63}^\dagger$, $\underline{70}^\dagger$, $\underline{77}^\dagger$, $80^\dagger$, $83^\dagger$, $85^\dagger$, 91*, 92*, $\underline{94}$*, 97*

Loire (Sweet W): $\underline{89}^\dagger$, $\underline{90}^\dagger$, $95^\dagger$, 96*, $\underline{97}$*, 98* Australia (NSW): $\underline{79}^\Delta$, 81^Δ, 84^Δ Australia (South): 79^Δ, 80^Δ, 84^Δ

7 = the best, - = not readily available, * = not ready yet, † = mature, Δ = drink soon Underlined are graded as 7's

R = Red wines W = White wines

Champagne : the festive drink

Champagne is the ultimate drink of celebration and consolation. At moments of happiness and triumph there is nothing quite like it. When times are hard it lifts your mood like no other drink can. And yet behind the froth is a remarkable wine made in a special place.

Centred on the cathedral city of Reims and the wine town of Epernay, the classic heartland of Champagne Viticole lies about 90 miles north-east of Paris on the road to the Belgian border. These are the most northerly fine wine vineyards in France. So frosty springs, variable summers and treacherous autumns pose potential problems to the quality and quantity of the grapes produced. Yet miraculously, the well-drained chalky soils of Champagne provide enough protection from the elements for the classic grape varieties to make juice which is rich in acids and sugar - the defining characteristics of a great sparkling wine.

Three grapes dominate the vineyards of Champagne. Pinot Noir, accounting for 37 per cent of total production, is planted mainly on the chalky sandy hillsides of the Montagne de Reims, giving wines of richness and body. The Montagne, more like a very large tree-topped hill than a mountain, dominates the skyline south of the city. The hardier Pinot Meunier is more suited to the frost-prone Marne Valley, where it produces regular crops of early maturing wine with a hint of spiciness - an essential and attractive component in a good non-vintage Champagne blend. Both Pinots are black grapes producing white wine (the skins are whipped away immediately after pressing so that the juice is not tinted by skin contact).

Chardonnay is the great white grape of Champagne. Delicate and fresh, with great aromatic potential, it is a vital component in the finer Champagne blends providing verve to balance the greater richness of Pinot Noir. The Chardonnay thrives in the deep Belimnite chalk of the Côte des Blancs. A lozenge-shaped barrier of hills that extends for 12 miles south of Epernay to the historic Mont Aimée, where the victorious English, German and Russian armies met after Waterloo.

The Champagne Method - or Traditional Method as Brussels insist we now call it - is the process of making a still wine sparkle by allowing it to ferment for a second

time in the bottle. It is now used to make superior sparkling wine around the world.

Outside Champagne, other producers of sparkling wines would have us believe that the method is all that matters, but what really matters is the wine and Champagne is unique. The skill of the blender puts it into a class of its own. Blending requires taste, experience and, above all, memory. The cellar master and his team in a great Champagne house will taste hundreds of still wines everyday in January and February following the vintage, eventually arriving at a selection of those that marry well with the established style of the house. The cellar-master will also call on reserve wines from older vintages to make up for any deficiencies in the present one. Well over 80 percent of all Champagnes are non-vintage; the best are aged for about three years before release and it always pays to give them another few months storage at home for greater mellowness of flavour.

Vintage Champagne. Every three to four years the top wine of an exceptional vintage is considered too good to be lost in the blending tanks. Good vintage Champagnes are aged for at least six years but are usually better still on their 10th birthday and beyond. For current drinking the hard-to-find 1990 can be magnificent, the 1993 is refined, subtle and classic; and just coming on stream is the 1995, which is likely to be a great long-lived vintage of exemplary balance.

Michael Edwards
Holder of Diplôme d'Honneur des Vignerons de Champagne
Winner of the Prix Lanson 1995

Bordeaux : the finest wine

The region of Bordeaux produces some of the world's finest red wines. Called 'Claret' by the English the wines are the result of a unique combination of climate, soil and grape varieties. The finest clarets come from estates (Châteaux) in the following areas:

1. The Médoc: on the west side of the Gironde estuary north of Bordeaux, and especially the land overlooking the estuary near the villages of St Estephe, Pauillac, St Julien and Margaux.

2. The Graves: the gravelly land just south of Bordeaux on the West Bank of the Garonne river.

3. St Emilion and Pomerol: the region east of Bordeaux near the town of Libourne on the Dordogne River.

A fine claret is always sold under the name of a Château or Domaine rather than an individual vineyard. Unlike Burgundy where only one grape, Pinot Noir, is used for the finest red wines, Claret is made from a blend of several varieties:

1. Cabernet Sauvignon: gives colour tannin and structure and imparts characteristic aromas of blackcurrant and cedarwood.

2. Cabernet Franc: lighter and more aromatic, gives elegance.

3. Merlot: gives softness, fruit and alcohol.

4. Petit Verdot: only used in small quantities, provides colour and finesse.

The exact proportion of each grape varies. In the Médoc and Graves Cabernet Sauvignon tends to dominate, in St Emilion, Cabernet Franc; in Pomerol, Merlot.

The wine sold under the Château label is called the 'Grand Vin' and is both a blend of grape varieties and of the best cuvées from different plots of vines. Not all a Château's production will be included in the 'Grand Vin'. Sometimes as much as 50% will be sold off under a second label e.g. 'Pavillon Rouge de Château Margaux" or as a 'village wine', e.g. St Julien.

At the time of the Paris Exhibition of 1855 the best wines of the Médoc were classified into 5 categories of growth (or Cru). Into the exalted company of first growths, Lafite, Margaux and Latour the Graves Château, Haut Brion was admitted exceptionally. In 1973 Chateau Mouton Rothschild was promoted from second to first growth. Otherwise this classification, based on price, and protected by law, has never been altered although often queried. These queries have arisen because the 1855 class-sification contains wines of excellence at all levels which on occasion can outperform those in higher categories. Among these are the so-called 'super seconds' such as Pichon Lalande and Ducru Beaucaillou, the third growth Palmer, the fourth Beychevelle and the fifth Lynch Bages.

No further classifications were made until that of Graves in 1959. This established no hierarchy between the classified Châteaux, but if one considers price and reputation the top performers are Haut Brion (already included in 1855) foll-lowed by La Mission Haut Brion, Domaine de Chevalier and Pape Clément.

St Emilion followed in 1969 with a classification of its wines into categories, revisable every 10 years. Top of the list here are Cheval Blanc and Ausone, both wines of great quality and a reputation to rival the Medoc first growths.

Finally, the Pomerol district remains unclassified although many of its wines are much in demand. But if price and reputation are the criteria then Pétrus easily tops the list, followed by Vieux Château Certan.

Classifications are, however, no more than a general guide to past performance and quality and there are always new discoveries to be made. The charm of claret is its variety and the opportunities it provides for encountering the unexpected.

The Right Hon. Sir Peter Emery P.C. Alex Paul

Truffles : the gourmet's choice

La Truffe "Le Diamant Noir" (Tuber Menalosporum or Tuber Brumale) is to haute cuisine what garlic is to Provençale cuisine and curry to Indian cuisine - one of the last mysteries the human being has yet to control entirely!

The truffle is the most precious of condiments that nature has given us to enhance the quality of certain produce mother earth provides, such as eggs, meat, fish, vegetables and pasta to name but a few.

In nearly 5 decades as a Chef Cuisinier from Maxim's in the 1960's and at the Connaught since the 1970's, I have used an average of 200 kilos a year of the best Tuber Menalosporum representing quite an amount of money at today's prices. I amuse people in saying that I could have bought the Dorchester nearly twice over in the 1970's with the money I spent on this most extraordinary fungus!

The harvest of truffles at the time of August Escoffier and Cesar Ritz (creators of haute cuisine and Grande Hotelerie at the turn of the 20th century) was in excess of a thousand tonnes annually. Nowadays it is between twenty and thirty tonnes and less in certain years. It is easy to understand why the truffle is so expensive now, due to the small harvest, when in the past it was so popular and quite affordable to use in cuisine.

It is one the most organic products known to man, and of course non-genetically modified, so hopefully the best allied to make haute cuisine palatable and refined.

Two great gastronomes of the Roman period, Lucullus and Apicius, praised the truffle as a unique gift from God. The Tuber Menalosporum (the black truffle) adapts beautifully to French cuisine while the Tuber Magnatum (the white truffle, only produced in Italy) is best suited to Italian cuisine.

The Middle Ages saw little evolution but the truffle was appreciated as a mysterious root by the peasant and from their discovery many noble families began to enjoy it.

During the 20th century due to the progress of communications and transport, the truffle began to be valued and much appreciated.

Truffles are still a mystery of nature. They cannot be cultivated although we can assist in providing the right environment for them to grow. Three main requirements are important for its development: a tree - Chestnut or Oak; the climate - Mediterranean; and the soil - very chalky.

I am very grateful to the three generations of the Pebeyre family: Alain, Jacques and Pierre-Jean who have helped me to appreciate "La Truffe du Perigord" and motivated me to create great dishes for the rich, the famous and the appreciative gourmet.

Here are four truffle dishes that I have created:

Consommé:	Consommé de Volaille "Prince of Wales" - Created in 1994 for HRH Prince of Wales on his visit to the Connaught. This is a consommé flavoured with truffle, chicken mousseline and root vegetables.
Egg:	Oeuf en gelée Stendhal (soft poached egg in aspic with truffle, ham, tongue and tomato mousse).
Game:	Tourte de Perdreau "Noce d'or" (leg of wild grey partridge, foie gras, savoy cabbage, truffle and puff pastry).
Fish:	Turbot Demi-Deuil (baked turbot and truffle, potato galette with cabbage and truffle).

Dr Michel Bourdin (Hon D. Lit)
Chancellor / Founder President of the Academy of Culinary Art
Maitre Cuisinier de France
Chef de Cuisine at the Connaught Hotel since 1975

Cognac : the perfect digestif

The origins of this noble drink are, in fact, quite humble. As with most great inventions cognac was discovered almost by accident. In the 16th and 17th centuries excess wine production in the Charente region meant that there were huge stocks of wine and this needed to be stored as buyers could not be found. The wine was therefore distilled and sold to the merchant navies of France, Spain and the Netherlands. It was discovered that the distilled wine aged quickly at sea and that the ageing had a very positive effect. Thus a new type of drink had been created. The drink took the name of the most important wine-trading city in the Charente region - Cognac.

During the following years the ageing process was developed into a fine art and, with blending, a well-balanced product was achieved. It was not until the 18th century that cognac became a chic and popular drink. It was brought to the fore by the 'café society' in London where it quickly became a favourite. With this popularity, cognac began to develop even further in terms of sophistication of ageing and blending. Large trading companies began to market their own brands of cognac, many of them from England and Ireland.

The producing region is today strictly regulated and defined. This region is in turn divided into six areas:
Grande Champagne is the 1er (first) Cru: this area is considered the source of the most delicate and aromatic cognacs and the designation will often be found on the label of estate cognacs. Grande Champagne is comprised of clay and compact, chalky soil (campanian chalk - hence the name Champagne).

Petit Champagne: surprisingly a much larger area than Grande Champagne. The "Grande" denotes the quality and amount of campanian chalk in the soil. Has many, but not all of the qualities of Grande Champagne. Fine Champagne may also be found as a designation on the label. This denotes a blend of eaux de vies from Petit and Grande Champagne (minimum 50%)

The other 4 areas are rarely mentioned on the label. They are Borderies, Fins Bois, Bon Bois and Bois ordinaires.

Eric Horwitz

Havanas : the ultimate cigar

Havana cigars are unmistakable in flavour, taste and aroma due to Cuba's unique soil and climate, as well as the heritage of knowledge of tobacco farming and the leaf itself. The first Cuban cigars (or Havanas) were 'discovered' by Christopher Columbus in 1492. Native Cubans enjoyed crude cigars, known locally as koheebas, made from twisted leaves of cured tobacco, held together by dried cornhusks. In the early 18th century, cigars more similar to those we smoke today were invented and being made in Seville with imported Cuban tobacco. This method of rolling was exported to Cuba in 1740, and with some encouragement from the Spanish King (by way of a royal decree) the seeds were sewn for what has become the best and most successful cigar industry in the world, a benchmark by which all others are measured, most aspire to and none have matched.

By the middle of the 19th century cigars were popular all over Europe, with Spain, and Britain being major importers, manufacturers and consumers. Despite the production of cigars using Cuban tobacco all over Europe, the imported cigar, the 'real' Havana, became a status symbol. Different shapes and size cigars were commissioned by wealthy Europeans, which later moved into the public domain and remain popular cigar sizes.

Wrapper leaves (capa) are the outside leaves that determines the cigars' appearance. It is one of the anticipatory pleasures of any cigar smoker to inspect the wrapper of a cigar that he or she smokes, to ensure that it is to their taste.
Binder leaves (capote) bind the filler in place and give the cigar its shape and size, and are a workmanlike leaf, also aiding in combustability.
Filler leaves (tripa) determine the flavour of a cigar, basically a balance struck between various types of leaf in order to produce the desired flavour.

Age refines the flavour of the finished cigar. A freshly made Havana is an entirely different smoking experience to one that has been matured. It is widely believed that Havanas should be smoked within a month or so of being rolled, or left to mature for at least a year. About five years maturation is considered optimum. When the cigar's fermentation is complete, its unique flavour is realised as was intended. In ideal conditions, cigars may be kept and matured virtually indefinitely.

Sami Sarkis

Three Gourmet Trips through Europe

What could be more pleasant than to travel by car from Northern Europe to the sunny Mediterranean whilst stopping for some superb meals en route. Living as I do in London, and having also lived in Scandinavia, I have made many car trips to the south and I thought my readers would like to benefit from my experience and knowledge of good restaurants along the way. I have chosen three different starting points but one can of course choose many other places in the north that can tie in with these routes. All stops suggested are listed in this guide. Do look at the individual reviews. Here we go:

Trip One: London - Côte d'Azur

Day One

After you have crossed the channel your first stop should be the three star Boyer Les Crayères in Reims. To get there you take the A26 motorway from Calais or Boulogne and the trip takes 3 hours. If you make a very early start from England you might get to Boyer for lunch but why rush - my suggestion is to have a light lunch on the way and get there late afternoon in time to walk in the lovely garden and then enjoy a sumptuous dinner and stay overnight. Warning: Boyer has only got 19 rooms so do book ahead.

There is an alternative to the first part of the journey. If you are only arriving in France late afternoon you could go for the first night to Château de Montreuil in Montreuil which is less than an hour away and then dine and spend the first night there and catch up the next day.

Day Two

Before leaving Reims do visit a champagne cellar or

two. This is a very interesting experience and can be arranged by the hotel. Let's assume you are not rushing and that you would only leave Reims late morning, driving south on the same motorway A26 towards Troyes.

The perfect place for your second night in France is hotel/restaurant Lameloise in Chagny in Burgundy. This is a small hotel in the centre of town and the restaurant is one of the best in France with three stars. Chef/patron Jacques Lameloise will look after your culinary needs.

Day Three

Now we travel through Burgundy on the A6 motorway (Autoroute du Soleil) down to the Rhône area. The choice for accommodation and dining is overwhelming once you are near Lyon but I have chosen two alternatives; one being Alain Chapel in Mionnay, north east of Lyon, and the other Pyramide in Vienne, south of Lyon. Alain Chapel is reached by taking off from the A6 north of Lyon and taking the A46 motorway spur; you will find Mionnay after 25 kms. To find Pyramide you should continue past Lyon on the A7 motorway southbound for 30 kms. Both have good 3 star restaurants and for accommodation Alain Chapel has 12 rooms and Pyramide has 21 rooms.

Day Four

On day four we drive into Provençe where there is a rich choice of places to eat and stay. I have chosen Oustau de Baumanière in Les Baux, one of the finest Relais & Chateaux in France. Beautifully located in the Valley of the Dead in Les Baux. The surroundings are sensational and the food is of good two and a half star level.

Day Five

At this stage most travellers from the north travel through Provençe and on to the Côte d'Azur where the choice is immense. Let me pick just one lovely spot and that is the Château de la Chêvre d'Or in the ancient rock village of Eze with a fabulous view over the Mediterranean and a small rock swimming pool. The restaurant has recently reached two star level. You will now have had a relaxing trip without rushing with five wonderful meals and after your dinner at Chêvre d'Or it is time to take a couple of days to relax by the sea.

Trip Two: Amsterdam - Côte d'Azur

Day One

What could be easier than driving directly south on the motorway from Amsterdam to Brussels. But why? I will tell you: to lunch in possibly the finest restaurant in Benelux, Comme Chez Soi in Brussels. After a delicious lunch, cooked by Pierre Wynants and his brigade, and eaten in the art nouveau restaurant, continue at a leisurely pace to Noirefontaine in southern Belgium, only 150 kms south-east of Brussels, mostly motorway. There you will find a charming inn, Auberge du Moulin Hideux. Have a relaxed dinner and spend the night there.

Day Two

Start fairly early, go back to the motorway and drive south into France and down to Strasbourg. This should take about 31/2 hours. Choose either of the three star restaurants, Buerehiesel or Au Crocodile for a fairly light lunch, and then take a look at the city of Strasbourg. This afternoon you only have to drive 65

kms to your dining and overnight stop which is one of the finest Relais & Chateaux restaurants in France, the Auberge de l'Ill, beautifully situated on the River Ill. The restaurant has a hotel annexe, where you can spend the night.

Day Three

Leaving Auberge de l'Ill, you head south and at Mulhouse you change motorways and go south west on the A36 in the direction of Macon, heading for Vonnas on the A40. In Vonnas you will stay at Georges Blanc, with wonderful food and a fine swimming pool.

Day Four

Going back to the Autoroute de Soleil (A7) head towards Avignon, taking exit 26 at Senas and the D973 towards Pertuis and the Luberon valley. Your destination is Lourmarin and the 18th century mill, Le Moulin de Lourmarin, a delightful two star hotel and restaurant.

Day Five

Continue at a leisurely pace through Provençe and to the Côte d'Azur. From many superb hotels I have selected the famous La Reserve in Beaulieu, which is of a very high standard both in accommodation and food, and has a large swimming pool. Now you can really relax.

Trip Three: Copenhagen - Côte d'Azur

Day One

This journey starts in Copenhagen, which is a good starting point, not only for residents of that city but for the whole of Scandinavia and Finland. People from the Nordic countries are great motoring tourists and as they have to cross the water to the continent usually drive via Copenhagen down to Rödby and take the ferry to Puttgarden in Germany, so this trip applies to all Scandinavian residents. After arriving in Germany drive straight to Hamburg where your first overnight stop will be the superb Vier Jahreszeiten Hotel and you can dine in their grill room overlooking the Lake Alster.

Day Two

Staying in Germany head south on the motorway down to Cologne which will take about 3-4 hours depending on traffic. In Cologne you leave the motorway and cross the Rhine heading up into the hills to Bergisch Gladbach where you are staying at Sclosshotel Lerbach. This is a small castle hotel with pleasant gardens. The restaurant is called Dieter Müller and I can assure you that you will have one of the finest meals imaginable.

Day Three

Start fairly early as we now have quite a long trip, but your final destination is a small hotel on a lake with one of the finest restaurants in the world. Go back to the motorway and head directly south via Karlsruhe down to Basel, Bern and Geneva. This is a fairly long journey but obviously if you feel like stopping overnight halfway you can. Arriving near Geneva, go round the

town on the motorway and head south into France towards Annecy. There should be no problem if you are good at map reading! At Annecy go through the town and head out to the lake on the left bank. After about 15 minutes you will arrive at Veyrier-du-Lac, where you will find Auberge de l'Eridan, a charming small hotel right on the lake. There are only nine rooms and two suites so do book well ahead. The hotel is closed from December 1st to March 20th. The most important reason to stay here is that chef/patron Marc Veyrat is one of the greatest chefs in Europe today. My wife and I recently enjoyed one of the finest meals we've ever eaten here. The next morning we swam in the lake.

Day Four

As you may wish to relax a little in the morning, this day you will have a fairly short journey on the motorway south via Grenoble to Valence. You will be staying at the first class hotel/restaurant Pic in Valence. They also have a limited number of rooms so please book well in advance.

Day Five

From Valence continue south on the motorway via Avignon and Aix-en-Provence towards the Côte d'Azur. Out of the vast choice I have once again chosen a rather special place and that is La Bastide St-Antoine on the hill on the outskirts of Grasse. Chef/patron Jacques Chibois cooks to a very high standard. The hotel has only got 11 rooms so once again book before you start your journey. There is a charming swimming pool.

French menu terms in English

Fish

Acarne	Sea bream
Aiglefin	Haddock
Anguille	Eel
Barbue	Brill
Brochet	Pike
Cabillaud	Cod
Carrelet	Plaice
Encorneu	Squid
Esturgeon	Sturgeon
Espadon	Swordfish
Flétan	Halibut
Lotte	Monkfish
Loup de Mer (also Bar)	Seabass
Merlan	Whiting
Merlu	Hake
Omble Chevalier	Arctic Char
Perche	Perch
Poulpe	Octopus
Rouget de Roche	Red Mullet
Truite	Trout
Thon	Tuna
St Pierre	John Dory

Shellfish

Araignée de Mer	Spider crab
Coquille St Jacques	Scallops
Crabe Bleu	Softshell crab
Crevette Gris	Shrimp
Crevette Rose	Prawn
Ecrevisses	Crayfish
Homard	Lobster
Huitre	Oyster
Langouste	Spiny lobster (clawless)
Langoustine	Dublin Bay prawn
Moule	Mussel
Oursin	Sea Urchin
Palourde	Clam
Tourteau	Crab

Game & Meat

Agneau	Lamb
Becasse	Woodcock

Becassine	Snipe
Boeuf	Beef
Caille	Quail
Canard	Duck
Coq des Bois	Blackcock
Coq de Bruyère	Capercailzie (wood grouse)
Dindon	Turkey
Faisan	Pheasant
Gelinotte	Hazelhen
Lapin	Rabbit
Lièvre	Hare
Oie	Goose
Palombe	Wood pigeon
Perdreau	Partridge
Poule de Neige	Ptarmigan (white grouse)
Tetras	Grouse
Venaison	Venison
Veau	Veal

Sauces

Aïoli	Mayonnaise with garlic & olive oil
Aurore	Tomato flavoured pink sauce
Bâtarde	Butter sauce with egg yolks
Bearnaise	Sauce with egg yolks, shallots, butter, white wine and vinegar
Bechamel	Creamy white sauce
Bercy	Sauce with white wine and shallots
Bigarade	Orange sauce
Bonne Femme	White wine sauce with mushrooms and shallots
Bruxelloise	Sauce with asparagus and eggs
Choron	Bearnaise sauce with tomatoes
Financière	Madeira sauce with truffles
Hollandaise	Butter, egg yolk and lemon juice sauce
Marchand de Vin	Red wine sauce with chopped shallots
Mornay	Cheese sauce
Mousseline	Hollandaise with whipped cream
Nantua	Cream sauce with crayfish and truffles
Talleyrand	Truffle sauce with cheese and foie gras

MAP - EUROPE

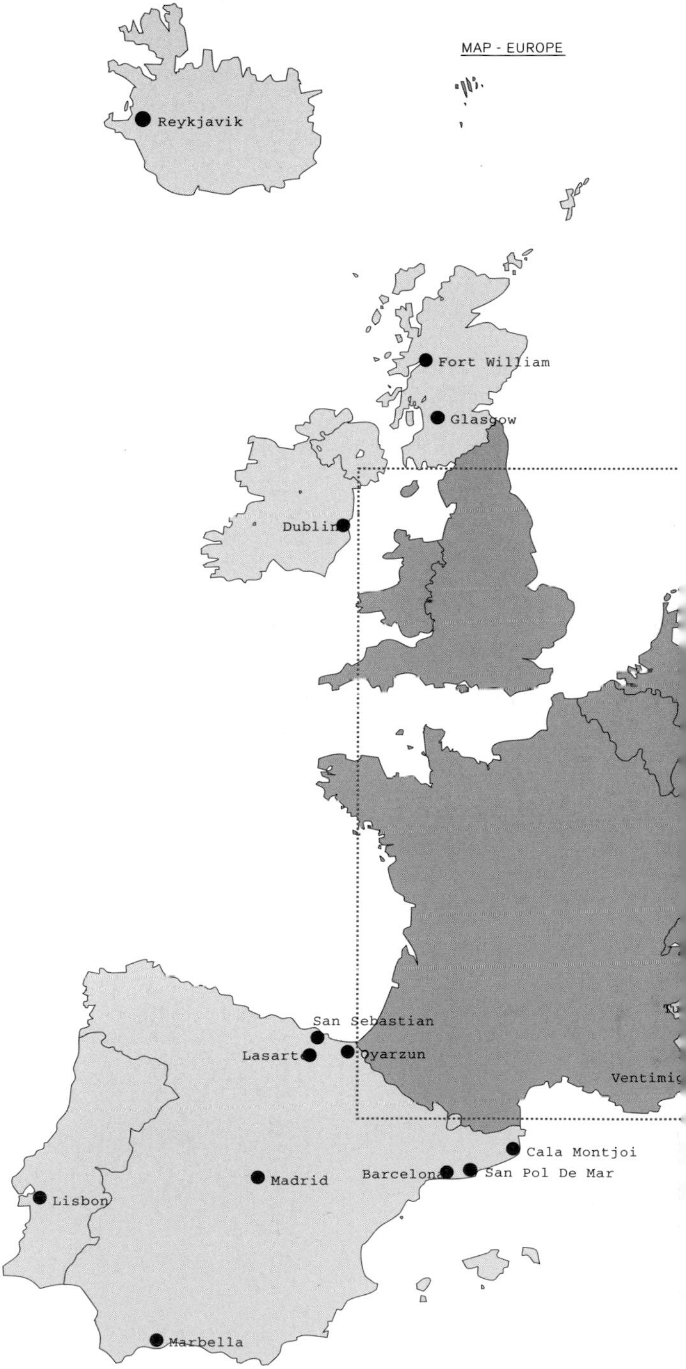

Reykjavik
Fort William
Glasgow
Dublin
San Sebastian
Lasarte
Oyarzun
Cala Montjoi
Barcelona
San Pol De Mar
Madrid
Lisbon
Marbella

Oslo
Stockholm
Helsink
St Petersburg
Moscow →
Gothenburg
Malmo
Warsaw
Prague
Vienna
Salzburg
Werfen
Budapest
Cernobbio
Erbusco
Venice
Canneto sull'Oglio
Chiavari
Florence
Porto Ercole
Rome
Sant Agata
sui Due Golfi
Skiath
Athens
Pireu
Vouliagmeni

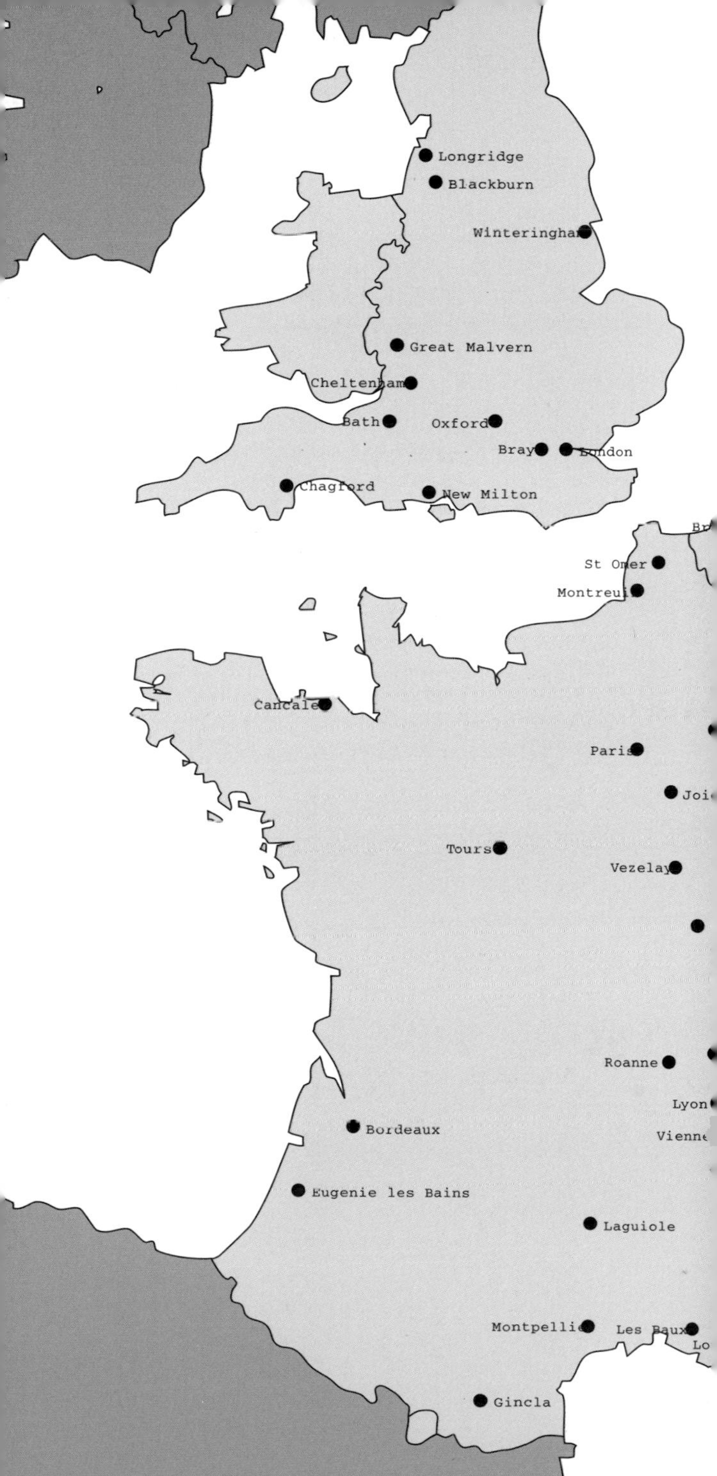
Longridge
Blackburn
Winteringham
Great Malvern
Cheltenham
Bath
Oxford
Bray
London
Chagford
New Milton
St Omer
Montreuil
Cancale
Paris
Tours
Vezelay
Roanne
Lyon
Vienne
Bordeaux
Eugenie les Bains
Laguiole
Montpellier
Les Baux
Gincla

MAP - CENTRAL EUROPE

Ordering Copies

North American sales and information:

Biblio Distribution
A division of National Book Network, Inc.
15200 NBN Way
Blue Ridge Summit
PA 17214
USA
Tel: 0800-462-6420
Fax: 0800-338-4550
E-mail: custserv@nbnbooks.com

European sales and information:

Portfolio Books Limited
Unit 5
Perivale Industrial Park
Perivale
Middlesex UB6 7RL
England
Tel: +44-20-8997-9000
Fax: +44-20-8997-9097
E-mail: info@portfoliobooks.com

Nordic countries sales and information:

Adrienne Florman
Florman Guides
Jungfrugatan 6
114 44 Stockholm
Sweden
Tel: +46-8-660-2525
Fax: +46-8-660-5310
E-mail: adrienne@flormanguides.com

Personalised editions:

Companies wishing to order personalised editions should contact Florman Guides at adrienne@flormanguides.com. Guides are available in quantities of 200 or more with your company's logo printed at the bottom of the front cover.

Symbols and organisation

Symbols

★★★	Outstanding cooking and service
★★1/2	Just below the very best
★★	Excellent cooking and service
★1/2	Approaching excellence all round
★	Very good quality
O	Good quality
FF	A Florman Favourite

Organisation

Guide organisation: entries are organised by country, with the capital city ranked first, and then by alphabetical order of both town and restaurant. Most restaurants are reviewed in full with others of quality (identified under the sub-heading 'Also recommended') also listed. Readers can identify all locations listed by referring to the maps at the end of the guide: if a town is marked then at least one restaurant from that town has been chosen for the guide.

Readers should be aware that the restaurants featured represent a personal selection of Europe's best restaurants along with a selection of other unusual and special restaurants known personally to the author (a 'Florman Favourite').

The guide is independent in its editorial selection and does not accept advertising, payment or hospitality from listed establishments.

The Florman Guide to
Europe's Best
Restaurants

D0547611

Published in Great Britain in 2001 by The Florman Guides
Limited, 24 Thurloe Square, London SW7 2SD

Editor Mark Florman
Marketing Adrienne Florman
Editorial assistant Annabel Florman
Production and design Marianne Kaplan AB, Sweden
Coverphoto Wolfgang Kleinschmidt
Maps Photodisc; K, C & T

Printed and bound in Finland by Sanoma WSOY

ISBN 0-9539625-0-4